Embrace Your Psychic Gifts

The Guide to Spiritual Awakening

Deborah Sudarsky, M.ED.

Embrace Your Psychic Gifts
The Guide to Spiritual Awakening

Difference Press, Washington, D.C., USA

ISBN: 978-1-68309-243-8

Cover Design: Jennifer Stimson
Editing: Bethany Davis

To my team of Earth angels, Robert, Luke,
Liv, and Lola

Table of Contents

Prologue 9
Chapter 1 You Are Here for a Reason 11
Chapter 2 My Story 15
Chapter 3 What Is Possible? 27
Chapter 4 What Is Psychic? 35
Chapter 5 What Are My Psychic Gifts? 41
Chapter 6 Being a Lightworker 61
Chapter 7 Consciousness 65
Chapter 8 Clearing 73
Chapter 9 Protection 79
Chapter 10 A Practice of Gratitude 83
Chapter 11 The Importance of a Meditation Practice 87
Chapter 12 Modern Day Tools 103
Chapter 13 What Now? 113
Chapter 14 Dealing with Challenges 117
Chapter 15 Conclusion 121
Acknowledgments 129
About the Author 131
About Difference Press 133
Thank You 135

Prologue

This book is intended to help people get in touch with their own unique gifts.

Chapter 1

You Are Here for a Reason

Have you ever started to wonder whether you were psychic? Do you have extraordinary intuition? Do you know when things are going to happen before they do? Do you see light and darkness on the calendar before an event? Perhaps you are starting to worry about your mental and physical stress because you don't understand what is happening. You see and feel things that others around do not register. Sometimes this makes you feel like you really are nuts! You've started to google esoteric terms because nothing is able to explain what is happening. You try and talk to your friends and family about things that have been going on, but they just shake their heads. You don't want them to be concerned, but you are experiencing things that just don't make sense. How is it that you can feel your co-workers emotions more than they do?

- Here are some signs that you might be psychic:
- You can feel what's going on with people and or feel a singular emotion in a room with strangers
- You can see energy around other people
- You can hear voices talking, but don't see anyone – and it makes sense to you
- You can feel or see things about people, places, and things that you have no reason to know
- You can locate water in a field using a rod
- You can feel a current of energy creating thoughts that are more informed about things than you know
- You can look at someone and know what is going on inside their body and the source of their medical conditions

If you have been researching any of these psychic phenomena and are wondering what is happening with you, then you have come to the right place. It sounds like you are having a spiritual awakening of some kind and it may be terrifying. Maybe what you have been experiencing contradicts everything you have been taught in your family or in your religion. This was certainly true for me. In this book, I will teach you to identify what is happening. You will figure out exactly how you are beginning to see, hear, or sense differently than others. We will demystify the mystical. We are going to use a questionnaire to help you identify your special skills and put names to things that you don't understand.

I will also discuss weird words, like "aura" and "chakras," that you may have heard but thought were only for the wacky, bizarre, and fringy characters from the outskirts of society. As it turns out, some of those terms can be really useful to know!

This book is going to show you that you are not alone and your suspicion that you may have some identified intuition can be utilized in a positive way. You may get a sense or feel "guided" to certain things or conversely, you may get a clear "don't go" somewhere. Maybe you have had a strong intuition in the past and didn't listen. Later you learned that it was a good lesson to follow your hunches. Maybe what you are feeling goes beyond a strong "gut" instinct. I want to clarify that I am not talking about fortune telling here. I actually don't believe that future events are predestined. I believe that we can change what happens with our intentions and our positive vibrations.

When I first started understanding that I had different abilities than the norm, I was so confused. I felt that being "spiritual" meant that I had to live in an ashram and forsake all of my material possessions. I thought that it meant I had to be poor. I was so bewildered by all of the material that I was reading. I wanted to understand how to use my skills but also wanted to be assured that I could live in today's world. I wanted to know that I wasn't crazy. I wanted desperately to be me and I was so confused about whether I would have to change in order to utilize my abilities.

In this book, I will discuss how you can coexist in the world with your special gifts. In fact, the world needs you just as and where you are. You are here for a reason. You have special talents that are necessary for this time. We need what you are here to do and all of the special qualities that you bring forth at this juncture. I am so excited about sharing this process of discovery with you!

Chapter 2
My Story

I grew up the youngest in a very traditional family. We were taught to have Ivy League aspirations and anything less was considered undesirable. My parents were both powerhouses. Dad was thoughtful and deliberate, and Mom had a lightning speed mind. Dinner was a discussion of world events and Dad sometimes discussed nuances between different vocabulary words. He was a lawyer and words mattered. We did not discuss our emotions on any topic, let alone spirituality. The world was the news, and the newspaper was sacrosanct. I tell you this because the backdrop for me learning about my special abilities meant defying everything that I was taught to believe. To my family growing up, the world was only what you could see.

From a very young age, I could read people. It always surprised my mom that I could tell what was going on with someone. It wasn't anything I learned in school, I just could see. I knew whether they were happy, or I could sense if they had issues. Sometimes I was able to identify someone's sadness. Mom would tell me that I was able to tell things about her friends that she hadn't even realized. I hadn't developed my special sight at this point, but I was always interested in psychology and what made people tick. Later, this developed into my interest in counseling work and wanting to help people.

I also had a host of invisible friends. We moved from a neighborhood with tons of kids to one where there were fewer playmates around. I would go to the local park and play on the swings and talk to my "invisible friends." Looking back I realize that this was the beginning of my interacting with the non-physical.

I was obsessed with believing that there was more to life than what meets the eye. I was consumed by what happens after we die. This was especially difficult growing up in a family like mine where we never discussed death. I remember walking home from school with my siblings and seeing a dead squirrel on the road, crushed by a car. That image haunted me for a long time, and I remember a dream that night about being at the pyramids in Egypt. I don't really understand the dream other than remembering the feeling like I had transported there. Since I was under five, it's hard to imagine remembering a dream from that time, but I have never forgotten it or the squirrel that inspired it. That dream really stayed with me and always reminded me that there was more to life than what meets the eye. The vivid colors and the gigantic pyramids felt so familiar. I knew early on that there were unseen elements affecting us all.

Since I was the youngest in my family, "I was to be seen but not heard." That meant I really felt that I had no voice. My family did not validate whatever I saw or sensed. And since they were all so successful, it meant that they were right and that maybe there was something wrong with me. I felt some shame that I saw the world differently. I wondered why I wasn't normal.

It was during my senior year in college that I finally had some validation. There was a class offered in the psychology department called "Altered States of Consciousness." The textbook we used was by Charles Tart. He explained the many layers of consciousness and psychic phenomena. Because this class was taught at a college level, it seemed credible. An authority acknowledged in writing that altered states exist and I had a teacher who believed it as well. It was a most exciting time for me. Someone in authority that I respected believed in the supernatural. It confirmed my every suspicion.

I was on the path to graduate school and getting a PhD in psychology. I knew that I wanted to work with people classified as schizophrenic and help them find normalcy. I worked in a mental health clinic helping people detoxify from alcohol and seek treatment, and for a suicide hotline. After that, I worked for the state of Vermont as a rehabilitation counselor in a halfway house, where patients were leaving the state hospital and needed some transitional time before living independently. It was here that I met some extraordinary people, patients as well as staff. The head of the facility was a priest and he was extremely open-minded and receptive. It was there that my learning really began.

One of the staff members told me about a psychic who read a Ouija board while talking to "Zuni Indian Guides." This sounded so exciting. I wanted to find out about my relationship and get some advice. I wondered whether we were meant to be together. That's really all I cared about at the time. I was told to bring questions, and again, I was mostly interested in my current relationship. I was introduced to the psychic reader and she appeared normal. She had blonde hair, blue eyes, and a gentle voice. She was a trained therapist and looked older than me, which made her seem more authoritative. The reading took place in my friend's house. I don't remember anyone else there, but I do know that when it was my turn it was only just the two of us. She and I sat down at a table with the Ouija board. I had seen one before when I used to play with one in my friend's basement. We had never taken it seriously.

Before she started, she told me a little bit about what would happen. She would do a prayer at the beginning and then the Guides would talk. After that, she said that I would have time for my questions. She didn't really explain the Guides other than that they were Zuni Indians. She said a prayer of protection in a soft voice and then started talking forcefully and decisively. Her earlier gentle manner had changed, and she had a completely different demeanor. She seemed more in command. Her hand glided over the board using the planchette, the heart-shaped piece of wood that marked the letters, so quickly that I have no idea how she was able to read the letters. I was mesmerized. You can only imagine how surprised I was when she started to talk. She spoke in rather halted English. "You are one of us," I was told by the Zuni Guides. "You are here to channel our energy on Earth." *Wait*, I wondered, *what?* I was one of them? She spoke in a very different voice and the words came out in a very fluid way. I was always interested in psychic phenomena but had no idea that I could have access like this. Were they kidding? Was this real? In my mind, this immediately acknowledged that there was life beyond this physical existence. I never doubted her credibility. These guides were speaking so fast and unlike the woman who channeled them. I knew it!!! But it was also terrifying and contradicted everything I was taught to believe growing up. What did this mean about my religion? What did this mean about world events? What was going on?

They told me that I could see auras and their colors and that I needed to practice. I didn't know that an aura was the energy field that surrounds the body. They also told me all the meanings for the colors: green meant physical healing, yellow meant mental energy, bright red meant anger, deep red meant passion, orange meant courage, brown meant energy that was stuck, and white meant spiritual energy. I didn't know if these colors were universal or whether they were just for me. I was supposed to start looking at people and allow this "sight" to develop. I was to look in their chakras, a word I hadn't known about, which they taught me. Chakras are seven energy centers in the body where energy flows.

The entire time they didn't even talk about my boyfriend! This was not at all what I expected to hear – and I really wanted to hear more about that boyfriend!

In the following weeks, I enlisted all of my friends and used them as guinea pigs. I also looked at my work clients, too, to see if I could see their colors. It actually started to happen – I could see colors! The chart of interpretations really made sense, too. If someone was really overthinking, the area around his or her head was yellow. When someone was extremely angry, I would see a bright red. Once, I saw a woman who had brown all around her. I didn't know her, but I felt that she wanted me to see this. I knew that it meant that she was physically not well. I wanted to know if my sight worked with people who were not as open. I later learned that I needed to ask for permission, that I couldn't just use my special sight without a person's knowledge. This actually made me feel better because I was protecting the person as well as myself from invading someone's being. I liked that the Guides were so thoughtful and seemed to have a very clear system in place. This also made me feel less overwhelmed. I wasn't ready to just see everyone's colors like this. I didn't know how to use this information at this point.

I continued to go see the psychic for subsequent visits. Each time, the Guides would reveal something new. I was told that I could see past lives. The Guides wanted me to practice in the same way, looking at people and seeing if I could see a different wardrobe or sense a different time. It all happened so quickly. The Guides talked to me about my third eye, which is the area in the middle of one's forehead above the brows. The third eye is one of the chakras; it opens our sight into the spiritual realm. We were working on opening that center so that I would have increased sight. The Zuni Indian Guides were training me to be a healer.

One minute I was ready to move forward in my career, getting a degree in psychology, and the next I was able to see colors around people and find out about their past lives. I didn't even understand what a past life meant! What exactly does it mean to have a past life, and for what reason was I being trained to see them? If I could see past lives, did this mean that there was reincarnation? Were we constantly reincarnating along a linear path? I asked the Guides this at one of my readings and they said no. We are not living a linear life, according to the Guides. We are living our lives simultaneously. Our minds separate linear time because otherwise it would be overwhelming. This was all challenging my everyday beliefs. And yet despite that, I knew it was all true. It had to be. I felt so good after each of my sessions! I felt more peaceful having these pieces of the puzzle come together. With each thing that I learned, I had so many more questions to ask.

I really never knew that I had this ability to see people's colors or past lives. And yet, once it was pointed out to me, I did start to see things. It was learning in a safe environment that made it possible. The psychic graduated from using the Ouija board, to just speaking directly to me when doing her readings. She was moving and growing, as was I. She put a group together of some of her clients and we met regularly. She would address us collectively and then give each of us information about our past lives and how they were affecting our present experience. It was an incredible time. We were learning about areas where we were stuck. The people in the group were all from very different backgrounds and yet we all collectively believed in the power of the Guides and the miraculous information that was coming forth. Many in the group were also counselors interested in personal development.

During my first reading, the Guides discussed one of my past lives. I was living in Peru on a high mountaintop, and had many children. They all perished in an earthquake, and I was completely devastated for the entire lifetime. Apparently, I was so overwhelmed that I could never grieve, and was completely stunted. What was fascinating to me was that in this lifetime, I had just started therapy. In therapy, we were discussing how I never allowed myself to be sad. I had never cried. I held in everything. I also knew how much I wanted to have children and a family. It all connected. It was so interesting to understand how past lives interact with the dynamics of our current lifetime. There was a lot to learn and explore with value for understanding what was happening in the present. I started to realize that there was a lot to learn about using past lives as a way to more deeply understand current relationships and experiences. It began to make sense that there were opportunities to heal by exploring previous lifetimes, understanding how they affect our current reality. By training me with reading colors and past lives, the Zuni Guides were expanding my knowledge, which in turn helped develop my work with others.

As I progressed with my studies, I was feeling the channel to the Guides strong enough to start doing readings for clients. It sort of just started to happen. I could hear them before I would speak my own words. It was a very interesting process where I would get into a meditative state but also be aware that something greater than me was having access to my vocabulary. I never felt afraid. Instead, I felt tremendous peace. I was following along but I wouldn't remember details when it was over. It was almost as though someone else was using my body and my mind in a very co-creative way. I really enjoyed the process and never felt tired. I will definitely explore this further in the book for those of you who want to learn how to interact with your Guides in this way.

I started working with clients, both individually and in groups, channeling the Zuni Indians. Through the psychic, I had a connection in NYC who would set up readings for me. It was incredibly dynamic and exciting. People were very excited about talking to the Zuni Indian Guides and my days in the city were filled. One thing that did bother me was that clients would come in and forsake their own guidance system. It was as though they had lots of questions and they just wanted answers. In a way, it was like me at the beginning – "Should I stay with this guy or not? You tell me, oh sacred Guides." People would ask very private questions and have high expectations that the Guides would know what was best. I always made it clear to my clients that if the answers didn't truly resonate with them, they should disregard any information. They themselves really knew what was best. However, it became clear that people come to psychics to get answers, not to look deep within themselves for inner guidance. I was not comfortable with that relationship.

I expanded my learning to start working on the body. I studied shiatsu, massage therapy, crystal healing, polarity healing, and cranial work. I loved working with the body, and I was so excited when emotional material would be released as we were working. I had one client who released so much that she lost a lot of weight and became so much lighter emotionally. When I would touch her, she would remember a significant event and it would trigger some emotion. We would work together on releasing blocks. She was so responsive. It really had an impact and confirmed my decision that getting a PhD in psychology was not the route for me. I loved how this realized immediate positive change. My experience working with the state hospital patients showed me that they were really treated to continue to stay sick with medications and lack of understanding. Many of my earlier patients had never learned the value of the healing process, something that cancer patients were beginning to learn from physicians like Bernie Siegel. Instead they focused on their disabilities and medications and were trapped in a recurrent cycle of repeated hospitalizations. I'm sure there are some really talented therapists doing good work but it became clear that it wasn't the right path for me.

The Zuni Guides were sharing new information. They spoke about things that I hadn't heard before, about energy and vibration. I was also very aware that I had to step back in order for the Guides to speak clearly. I wanted to make sure that my ego was out of the way. I realized that I was a prism for their ability to communicate. If I had an issue about something, it would block the transmission. It was very important for me to have integrity with the work. That meant working on myself, too. I wanted to be as clear as possible so that the transmissions weren't tainted by my ego.

The transmissions were clearly not coming from me. Although they were being expressed through me and used my words, I recognized that they were coming from a perspective way above me. I used to feel that the Guides were coming through me, but I later started to realize that I was elevating myself to their level. And this was when the work became even better. I wasn't just a vessel. As the Guides and I worked together, it became very comfortable. I had access to information that I wouldn't be able to explain otherwise.

I know it must seem that it would be incredible to have access to this information all of the time and that I was special. But I am here to tell you that each of you has come to read this because you have a desire to work at this level as well. You all have access to this work in your own unique way. Each of us has our own team of powerful guides. We will be exploring this throughout the book and hopefully demystifying it for you and making it more comfortable. Each of you has special skills that you are here to share and that will make a difference.

I will say that medicine has come so far from the early days when I was starting my practice. Doctors now understand that they need to work with the whole person, including their environment. They can't just treat symptoms. They now want to understand how everything fits together. If I had given in to my fears about what I was doing, I wouldn't have made a difference. But I feel that all of the early pioneers in holistic health contributed to changing medicine today. So when you start to identify some of your own special skills, recognize that you are making a difference, too. Even if things are uncomfortable, you will find your way with your skills and your abilities. You have these skills for a reason. You may be aware of them, or you may not. As we go forward, we will figure this out together.

Chapter 3

What Is Possible?

Up until this point, you have wondered whether you might have some psychic abilities but weren't sure. The thought actually caused you to feel terrified because you conjured up all of those scary movies and felt that it meant you would see horrifying events in the future. And because of that, you may have shut down. You may have felt that there was something wrong with you. It may feel like you can't tell your intimate relations that you have some of these special abilities because they will think that you are a freak, or even worse, that you are crazy. Believe me, many of my closest friends and family knew nothing about my psychic experiences because I also had concern about being labeled or judged. However, there are whole groups of amazing and loving people out there who will understand you and want to discuss this further. Your whole world will expand and some of the things that you have been worried about will begin to make sense. This can be a very exciting time!

Here is what we will be doing in the next chapters ahead.

In Chapter 4, I will discuss what it means to be psychic. "Psychic" is such a polarizing word with so many different interpretations. Many of you have come here to understand what is happening to you; others may know your gifts, but might be ignoring them. It is also important to understand how these gifts are the beginning of understanding the concept of spirituality and what that means for you.

In Chapter 5, I will discuss different aspects of being psychic. It is here that you will take the Exceptional Test to discover your own abilities. It may be that you share many different ways of being psychic and we will discuss the overlap and what that means. Keep in mind that all of this will shed light on becoming more awakened to the energies around you and help you learn how to develop your gifts.

In Chapter 6, you will learn that there is a higher purpose for learning about your psychic gifts and that you are part of a movement. In Chapter 7, we will discuss Consciousness and what it means. This is also when we will begin to explore what it means to be awakened spiritually.

In Chapter 8, we will begin to explore the difference between your energy and those around you. In Chapter 9, we will discuss ways of protecting your newfound sensitivities. Chapter 10 and 11 are about the importance of integrating two important practices into your lives: gratitude and regular meditation. In Chapter 12 we will discuss new tools to help support you on your journey and in Chapter 13 we will explore what comes next.

We will work together to find out your special skills. The Exceptional Questionnaire, in Chapter 5, will serve as a launching point for you to discover your own special abilities. Like in my story, it may not be until someone points you in the right direction that you know that these things exist. Maybe you have a suspicion but haven't pursued thinking about it because the whole thing just seemed overwhelming and no one around you would believe you.

Often people wonder what will happen if they are found out for having special psychic abilities. Maybe you are happy with the way things are and really don't want to open up Pandora's box. Will this mean having to change? I had so many preconceptions when things started happening to me. My biggest concern was wondering whether my being psychically aware or "spiritual" meant that I would have to forsake all material possessions. I was really at a crossroads, feeling that most of my psychic friends had issues with money and the material world. If I believe in the spirit world, then why did all of this matter? I have learned that actually being spiritual and interacting with the material world means even more. Just focusing on spirit and giving up on the material world is not what it is about at all. The understanding of all of this is really to enhance our lives and make them more meaningful. We are here to make a difference, not to live in a yurt praying to the Mud Gods!

If you are in a very corporate or traditional job, it may seem very bizarre to even discuss the possibilities of delving into the unexplored topic of psychic abilities, even if you are yearning to know more and to find out what's going on with you! The biggest worry I think is, will I have to change? Always when you learn a new skill or develop new interests, you change because your perspective is enhanced. Your education may lead you to meet new people and to take you down an unexplored path. You may find that you are reading different kinds of books and interested in different kinds of classes. However, at the core of all of this is you. Fundamentally, you are the source of all that you experience. These new skills will not change your core. If anything, they develop something that is a more specialized, unique aspect of you.

Oftentimes when we begin to feel a sense that we have some abilities or see things that are difficult to explain, we feel that things are out of control. We feel that we can't manage what's happening to us and that is terrifying. It feels as though there is some poltergeist dominating our thoughts and actions. However, it is very important to understand that we have jurisdiction over what happens to us. We can ask for things to slow down or speed up. The way we see the world is ultimately our decision. I know with my Guides, if I feel that things are happening at too quick a pace, sometimes I just have to say, "Slow down!" Things do not have to be scary or taken to a level at which I am not comfortable. The goal is to be comfortable and to feel that things are a positive expression. We are in the midst of transforming. However, the pace is totally in your hands. Please remember that you are in charge at all times. If you are not feeling that way at this moment, we will learn more as we proceed through different ways of understanding what is going on. Awareness and understanding help to process what is happening. And again, the pace is up to you.

We all have these senses: hearing, seeing, feeling, tasting, and touching. Now we're working on further developing your sixth sense, which is intuition. Some people have different ways of finding that sixth sense. As we explore this further, we will find out exactly what skills you have. Maybe you know what is going on at this point. Or, maybe you have inkling that you have different abilities than others but aren't sure exactly what is happening. As we proceed further, we will begin to nail down exactly what is going on with you. Learning what is happening takes a lot of the fear out of the process of what is unfolding. You are here because you sense that there is more for you to discover about yourself. You know that you have more going on at this time and you want to understand what is happening. Learning how to develop intuition is a huge part of this process and you will feel a stronger sense of guidance. This can feel like a rudder on a boat. It gives you a sense of stability and direction. Ultimately, it can really further that experience of a "gut" feeling that heads you in the right direction.

Some of you may feel a calling for the greater good. When you begin to explore that sense of what your abilities are calling for attention, you will see that maybe there is a unique way for you to offer help to others. In this way, your psychic abilities can start to be seen as gifts and not just as scary things happening out of control. Understand that your unique "sight" offers a way to help others in ways that many may not be able to do for themselves at this point. Learning your abilities gives you clarity. Clarity is so extremely valuable because it gives you the ability to navigate in a more purposeful and deliberate way. It helps you to rise above the everyday chaos of life and see. Clarity is often something that is valued by others when they can't see exactly what is happening. It's not only helpful on a personal level, but it can be extremely useful on a corporate level. It can help in schools, hospitals, or any setting where there is an organizational structure. Your ability to be clear offers a unique perspective. Being able to process on that very subtle level is extremely useful in settings where others may have lost their sight.

You may have found a desire to lead a more meaningful life. You have felt a longing to go deeper. You are recognizing that you have some kind of special gift and you want to find out what it means. You want to explore life beyond what it looks like on the outside. Your special gifts are calling you to pay attention. It may not always be what you think you want at this point, but upon further investigation you find that it is extremely satisfying. Learning and developing your innate abilities is another way to create value. This is especially true when you discover a sense of purpose that you had not recognized before. You are here for a reason. What is it that you are meant to do here at this time? These are some of the questions that we are going to address as we explore your unique abilities.

Finally, some of you are wondering how this might interact with your religion or faith. You wonder whether exploring psychic abilities contradicts all that you were taught to believe. Will this shake your faith? Are you going against the values and principles that you were taught and that are at the core of your own belief system? The principles that we will be exploring are meant to work in conjunction with your beliefs and understandings. We are hoping to find peace here. Learning that you have special skills means working within the system that is you. These skills are meant to enhance your abilities, not contradict them. Although my own psychic learning confirmed that I don't believe in death and that I believe in the spirit world, I find that it gives me an even deeper appreciation for my own religion. I actually have come to recognize the similarities in all religions and am comfortable with all beliefs, not just my own. This has opened up more compassion in my heart. Learning to see the universal principals in all religions gives one a sense of connection with humanity. These are some of the questions that we are going to address as we explore your unique abilities.

Chapter 4

What Is Psychic?

The word "psychic" is used in so many different contexts that now is a good time to discuss what it means. According to Google Dictionary, one standard definition of the word "psychic" is as an adjective. It means, "relating to phenomena that are inexplicable by natural laws especially involving telepathy or clairvoyance." The second meaning is a noun. "A person considered or claiming to have psychic powers: a medium, clairvoyant, fortuneteller, prophet, seer, soothsayer, forecaster of the future." My personal definition pertains to someone who has certain sensitivities to the supernatural or unexplained elements around them. It can mean someone who is able to interact with the non-physical through sight, touch, or sound. When I describe someone's psychic abilities, I mean someone who has a very particular way of intuiting the information around them. I mean those that respond to energies that are not visible to others.

What is the difference between your intuition and your psychic ability? Everyone is born with intuition. How often you use it or listen to its messages determines how accurate or detailed it can be. Taking your intuition and really practicing or honing its abilities is one way to further develop psychic ability. The more you practice using these skills, the more range you can develop. Like a musician, you can improve your skills with continued practice and repetition. Some people have a very finely developed intuition, but that doesn't mean that they are psychic. It means that they listen to that intuition.

Others have natural psychic ability. They were born with it and have been aware of it since they were little. Some ask for it to be shut down because it's too difficult to deal with at certain times in life. And the ability lessens as you use it less. However, if you choose to reactivate it, it will reassert itself exactly where you left off.

Two different people with psychic abilities may perceive things very differently and have very different skill sets. It is not a standard-definition word. When I think of the old school "psychic," it conjures up someone who sits in a séance and starts speaking with dead people. I think of someone who closes his or her eyes and forecasts the future. In this case, I am using the word "psychic" for lack of a better word. There really isn't a true definition for what it means, considering we all perceive things uniquely to us. However, in the context of this book, I am referring to psychic as a set of extraordinary skills where one is able to perceive things that others are not able to witness. Using psychic ability means being able to intuit with precision things unseen that are going on. Psychic means tapping into other dimensions and seeing things that are of extrasensory perception, whether through sight, sound, or kinesthetically. Those with psychic ability are able to tune into the spirit world. The spirit world feels as real as the three-dimensional world with sight, sound, and smell. By showing interest in this book, you are beginning to recognize that there is something about the way that you perceive things that is different from how others see the world. And it's causing concern because you see that you have different abilities from others. It may make you doubt yourself because not everyone validates the things you notice. And yet, when you are truly being honest, you absolutely believe what you are feeling. It's just hard because no one else sees what you are able to see. Perhaps you are comfortable with your abilities and just want to learn more. I know for me, when I am in a community with like-minded people it makes it easier for me to stretch my skills.

The word "psychic" is a blanket term. It covers a lot of grey area. I am specifically addressing a skillset that is unique to each individual here. Each of you is attuned very specifically to the world around you. You are here because you made the decision to have access to this skill set before you were born and recognized value in staying directly connected to the world beyond. What this means is that you have come to recognize that you perceive things in a way that those around you do not. It calls into question that you are seeing things that many may not see. This makes you wonder whether you are crazy because it's not often that you get directly validated. And yet, being psychic or perceived as psychic means learning to trust the information that you are getting, and recognizing the value and the timing for what you are feeling.

"Psychic" means knowing something is about to happen before it does. "Psychic" can also mean feeling something from another that they may not be feeling themselves. All of these terms mean psychic. Again, it's just a blanket word for experiencing things palpably that others might not know themselves.

Attunement is also another way to understand being psychic. It is a way of being totally focused and receptive toward another and receiving information.

Many paid soothsayers, palm readers, and psychic hotlines are those with zero ability to read the future. There are some "psychics" who I have encountered who know how to read thought forms. It appears that they are accurate because they are reading what's going on in your mind. It isn't the future that they see but a projection of your belief system about the future. Often afterward, you are blown away by what you think is someone's ability to see into the future.

During the time that I started to study with my Guides, I went to many psychics along the way looking for guidance and direction. I realized that there were many tricks that people used to seem as though they could read into the future. There are just many levels of skills and information. It was a great learning for me because I wanted to hear certain things being reinforced and was often disappointed when I didn't get to hear what I wanted. I learned that just because someone calls himself or herself psychic doesn't mean that they are picking up information that is useful. I learned that you have to be discerning about whom you listen to and what information is being shared.

Since those early years, I came to understand that the future is not set in stone. We live in a vibrational universe and it is always moving. This is why intentions are so important; because you create the path for things you want to have happen. So for those afraid of their psychic gifts, it is important to remember that the future is constantly changing. Sometimes just getting information and saying things aloud gives us an opportunity to pivot and create something new. Do not be afraid to explore your psychic talents because of some fear of the future. You are evolving and transforming at every moment and there is constant motion. Life is exciting and a blend of alchemy!

This book will discuss being psychic as possessing certain sensitivities and abilities that others around you may not have or understand. I am not talking about developing an aptitude for prediction. I understand that each of you may have already learned to develop some skills or may believe that there are skills that may be lying dormant. It is my goal to unearth these special qualities so that you may recognize ways of utilizing these gifts to further express your true self as well as contribute to the world around you.

Chapter 5

What Are My Psychic Gifts?

As we just discussed, there are so many different ways of being psychic. I am going to list several kinds of abilities, although if you don't see yourself in this list it doesn't mean anything. In fact, if you feel that your particular way of seeing is unique, then that is very exciting and you are at the forefront of your specialty! This is just a very loose guide.

This list includes:

- Empaths: The ability to feel and absorb the emotions of others
- Channeling: The ability to speak to non-physical beings
- Clairaudience: The ability to acquire information by hearing from non-physical beings

- Clairvoyance: The ability to perceive people, objects, or events via extrasensory perception
- Starseeds: Those that come from other planetary dimensions, recognizing that Earth seems unfamiliar
- Dowsing: The ability to locate water using a rod
- Aura reading: The ability to perceive energy fields surrounding people
- Medical Intuitive: The ability to decipher issues going on in the body

I've put together The Exceptional Questionnaire for you to review. In it, look to answer the questions from as easy a place as possible. The questionnaire is for you to begin to isolate the areas where you have been feeling you are different from others in terms of how you are processing information. These are things that give you the idea that maybe you are experiencing psychic perception. Hopefully, this will help identify your strengths and isolate what makes you different. As you learn to identify these gifts, they become less frightening as you see that there is purpose to what is happening at this time. Please check off as many answers as you can, which describe things that you have experienced. Put a check by the number, circle your answers, or write them down. This list of numbers will serve as a "key" to figure out which psychic abilities you may have. If you don't see yourself in this list, please understand that your desire to learn more may mean you have some talents ready for discovery.

The EXCEPTIONAL QUESTIONNAIRE!!!

1. When the phone rings, do you know who's on the other end before you answer?
2. Can you see colors around other people?
3. Do you hear voices that sound like conversation only no one is there?
4. Does technology come easy to you?
5. Do you dream about events that you think are part of your past from other lifetimes?
6. Can you see energies on the body and know what's going on?
7. Do you feel other people's emotions more than they do?
8. Do you feel energy coming from your hands?
9. Do you "just know" stuff about people and what they are feeling?
10. Can you hear what people are thinking?
11. Do you just know people's thoughts even though they may be saying the exact opposite?
12. When you look at the sky do you feel more connected to the stars?
13. Can you see people that others don't see?
14. Do you have flashes of events before they happen?
15. Does the Earth speak to you on the land and direct you to water?

16. Do you ever feel as though your blocks of thought are more intelligent than what you normally think?
17. Do you feel that you absorb other people's emotions?
18. Do you have issues with authority?
19. Do you see flashes of color?
20. When you close your eyes to meditate, do you have a clear sense of something that you need to do?
21. Do you look around and feel that this place doesn't feel like home?
22. Do you sometimes feel like speaking a language that you haven't heard before?
23. Do you connect on a deep level with animals?
24. Can you feel when the energy is stagnant in your apartment?
25. Do you feel a calling to working with a divining rod?
26. Can you hear what animals are thinking?
27. Does the Earth speak to you?
28. Do you rage against the status quo?
29. Can you walk in a room and feel what's going on emotionally?
30. Do you feel that you were meant for more?

If you have put a check by any numbers, this means you have some psychic ability. Chances are you might have resonated with more than one. I'll explain how there can be overlap later on in the chapter. Most importantly, this is a jumping off place to begin to think about how you see, feel, or hear things and how they may be your own special way of sensing the world around you.

EMPATHS:

You might be an empath if you checked "yes" in the Exceptional Questionnaire to any of the following questions: #5, 7, 8, 9, 17, 23, 29, 30

Many people with psychic abilities are empaths. Empaths are highly evolved people with extra sensitive abilities who feel the emotions of others. Often, empaths don't know that they have these abilities. They walk into a room and get bombarded by the emotional content of other people and don't know exactly what hit them. They may be at work and have a co-worker complain about a problem and then feel a physical sign of distress, like a headache or stomachache. Empaths are an incredible gift on the planet and come from a long line of healers. In ancient times, empaths were considered among the elite forms of healers for the refined skills they had. Being an empath is not something that can be learned. One can develop empathy. But being an empath is something that is decided before birth. This is a very specialized form of healer. We need empaths on the planet because they help to remind others that they are not alone. Empaths have the ability to touch people's hearts and create a sensation of connection. Most empaths find themselves in the helping fields because their higher mission is to help transmute emotional pain. They absorb others' pain in order to help someone feel better. It is an honor to be an empath.

Many people who are empaths feel that it can be a burden because they are often carrying around emotional content that may not belong to them and they don't know where it originated. If you are an empath and working in the healing profession using your skills, it makes it easier to understand what is going on. However, if you don't understand that you have these skills, you may be walking around taking on emotional stress without understanding how to process everything.

Empaths also have extremely vivid dreams where they often are in the center of groups of people and they actually can be working on the astral plane as well. The astral plane is the realm beyond the physical. They take on this role to help alleviate the negativity on the planet. It is a way of transmuting pain. Most empaths have lived many lifetimes as empaths and it is a role that they have chosen because it is a highest calling. Healers and the healing profession were revered in many cultures and it is a noble art.

Living during this time where there is so much chaos and dissent, it is not easy to be an empath. Many empaths feel a sense of burden about taking on so much emotion. It can be difficult to be so absorbent and to know exactly the best way to disperse the energy. Learning how to use this skill effectively is important in order to provide self-care. Empaths need to cleanse their energy fields often so that they are not recreating other people's issues. We live in a vibrational universe and clearing energy is very important for empaths. Without clearing, you may unintentionally create someone else's issues within yourself. We will discuss clearing later on in the book. Empaths often have other psychic abilities as well.

It is important to begin to identify and recognize if these qualities are something that you possess. Do you feel what others are going through more than they recognize themselves? Do you walk into a room and know exactly what the group is feeling? Do you feel as though you are drained and exhausted after someone you know unloads his or her problems? Can you be feeling really well and then, after someone walks by, suddenly have a downturn in energy? If you recognize any of these symptoms, you may be an empath.

Beginning to identify as an empath is the beginning of recognizing how to start to process this ability. We will talk further about tools for you, but start to pay attention if you are finding that you relate to the description above. It is something that can overwhelm you if you are not aware because just being in a public arena can mean picking up other people's emotions if you are not paying attention.

I have a client who would come to me every week with a long list of things to work on. However, we would spend most of the time clearing her energy because she was unaware that she was picking so many things up in her office. She worked in social work and there was a lot of emotional content in the office from clients and the workers assigned to helping them. Once she started to learn ways to clear her energy, we could start working on her goals of creating a private practice. Along with clearing, empaths need to learn about creating firm boundaries. This allows them to work with others without absorbing all of the emotional stuff that's being released. It is a lot easier to deal with communal living, offices, and traveling once an empath becomes aware of when they are taking on things that aren't theirs.

Empaths are in many fields. It doesn't mean that you have to change career paths and become a healer. In fact, being an empath is a gift to any organization. It means that you are able to identify what is going on emotionally, which can be a huge tool for making positive change in any environment. Starting to learn more about how you react to situations can help you learn how to navigate this world with these specialized sensitivities. We will go more into tools for protection and clearing later in the book.

CHANNELS:

You might be a psychic channel if you checked "yes" in the Exceptional Questionnaire to any of the following questions: #5, 8, 16, 20, 22, 23, 24, 27, 30

You may see some overlap with the answers for being an empath. Those that channel can also be empaths or have similar traits. These are just very loose guidelines. However, if you say "yes" to the answers for channels, it may be that you have some ability that we will explore about how to use your gifts.

As I discussed earlier in the book, I am a psychic channel. Because the Zuni Indians told that to me, I have always felt that's how I identify myself. When I think about my purpose here on Earth, I know that I am meant to channel positive energy on the planet. In any kind of situation, I call upon my Guides to bring light when it feels as though there is something negative going on. Let me elaborate more about what it means to be a channel.

Before I had my first reading with the psychic, I had absolutely no idea that I was meant to do this work. I knew that I was interested in psychology and helping people and I was also completely driven to learn what was in the beyond. I knew that there was more going on than meets the eye on the planet. I couldn't believe that we lived and died and that this was all there was. I knew that there was more for us here. Life was too complex to just have no understanding of an afterlife. So when I first was introduced to "the Guides," it totally made sense to me even though I never expected to hear that information. I didn't even question their authenticity because they seemed to know so much about me on such a deep personal level. Certainly the channel who was reading for me couldn't know me that way. And she seemed just as surprised by my reading as I did. So as skeptical a person as I was, this totally made sense.

If, according to your answers to the Questionnaire, you may be a channel, I think your Guides are leaving you clues along the way. You may feel a sense of connection to wanting to know more about spirituality. You may find yourself interested in psychic mediums or the tarot. Something may be driving you to learn more about your own connection to your spiritual family. Maybe there is an increased sense of desire. Leading up to my discovery that I was a channel, I was experiencing a strong connection to the supernatural. I was in school learning about altered states of consciousness and also learning to meditate. So even though it was a surprise, now that I look back, the dots connect. I was being prepared for this type of communication.

When I first started to work with my Guides, they actually talked through me. Now, I use the written word for my Guides to communicate with me. If you are interested in exploring this further, I suggest leaving a journal nearby for when you meditate or after a moment of alignment (dancing, walking the beach, or painting). Sometimes just writing what first comes into your mind is a chance for your Guides to communicate with you. As you continue this practice on a regular basis, the communications will get easier and you will recognize if it's your mind or really your Guides. I always know it is my Guides because their communications are at a whole other level from what I could write on my own. Sometimes, working with a likeminded friend is a wonderful way to explore this modality. When one person asks questions, the other person can see if they feel a transmission. I love working on the computer. I ask for protection and say a prayer where I ask that only good come to each and everyone and for all negativity to depart. I will often light a candle and take some time to go inward and align with the higher energies. After that, the words just start typing themselves.

When I first started channeling, my Guides often talked about earth changes. It was a recurrent theme and one that was mentioned to each client. At the time, there were occasional hurricanes coming from the Caribbean, but otherwise it was a foreign concept. Now, there are stories every day in the paper about tsunamis and earthquakes. My Guides may also have been forewarning each of us about climate change. When you get messages about recurrent themes, it is important to pay attention.

CLAIRAUDIENTS:

You might be clairaudient if you checked "yes" in the Exceptional Questionnaire to any of the following questions: #3, 10, 20, 23, 25, 30

Clairaudience is different from channeling. It means that non-physical beings are talking directly to you but not through you. It's as though you can hear actual conversations. Many commercial psychics work this way. They can hear things on the spirit plane. With channeling there is co-creation where one's vocabulary is being accessed. With clairaudience you are actually having conversations or listening to others who are non-physical. It is really important to note that just because you are listening to a non-physical being doesn't mean that they are on a high level of understanding. The spirit world is filled with entities like on Earth. Some spirits are those that I would never wish to engage with in conversation. We will talk about protection and guidance later on in the book, but if you are hearing spirits, it is important to make sure that you are able to discern whom they are and whether they are providing high-level conversation. If the voices that you hear are telling you to do destructive things and are frightening, it is important to seek the help of a professional counselor. High-level spirits speak in very positive messages. If you are hearing things that make you feel bad, then you may need some other kind of help. The voices from my psychiatric patients were always extremely negative and destructive. Those voices could mean that you need some help, especially if they are telling you to do harm to yourself or others. There are lots of mental health hotlines on the Internet and they are available 24/7.

CLAIRVOYANTS:

You might be clairvoyant if you checked "yes" in the Exceptional Questionnaire to any of the following questions: #1, 5, 9, 11, 13, 14, 20, 23, 24, 30

Clairvoyants are people who have extraordinary vision about past or future events. It is also a blanket term for most people with psychic ability. As you can see from the number of yes answers to the questionnaire, clairvoyants are able to combine many psychic gifts. Although the future is constantly changing, clairvoyants are able to see things with extraordinary clarity. Being clairvoyant is something inherent and not something that can be learned. While people with ESP can practice and cultivate the ability to use this talent, clairvoyants are naturally gifted. Those with this special gift of sight can sometimes feel overwhelmed and frightened that they are seeing things that they are not ready for. But it is important to recognize that you can control what you want to experience. If it is getting to be too much, you can tell your Guides that they need to slow it down. In the quiz, many qualities may be considered to be clairvoyant because it is sort of a blanket word to describe people who have a lot of ways of experiencing psychic ability.

STARSEEDS:

You might be a starseed if you checked "yes" in the Exceptional Questionnaire to any of the following questions: #4, 12, 18, 21, 23, 28, 30

"Starseed" may be a new and unfamiliar word. But, as I was putting this book together, my Guides underlined the importance of including starseeds at this time. Many millennials are starseeds. Many of you here now come from other planetary dimensions. You are called starseeds because you bring forth elements of other energies not seen here before. Starseeds defy convention, they can have super technological abilities, they heal quickly, and they can materialize thought quickly without having prior knowledge about a topic, making them seem like wizards. They are able to move forward big innovational ideas that we need on the planet at this time. Although their psychic gifts are not as easy to recognize, they are able to access information that might not normally be available. Innovations in science, medicine, and technology are coming from the starseeds. Most starseeds are here to advance the planet.

One of my clients is a starseed. I understood that when I met her because her energy was vastly different. She had a light quality and she vibrated on a faster frequency. I could tell that just by touching her and comparing her to other clients. We definitely had to work on grounding together. We used different exercises that cleared her energy and also connected her to the Earth. Nature was a very important healer for her, and part of her weekly practice was to find a park and walk around. She also processed things very quickly and I had to let her energy guide me, as my tools weren't always effective. We will talk about meditation later in the book and starseeds, like everyone, benefit enormously because meditation provides an opportunity to access information. She worked in technology where she was able to give enormous feedback to the CEO because she could analyze whether their new systems were effective. This was remarkable because she was one of the youngest employees at the company.

It is possible that you may possess several of the qualities that I just described. For example, many starseeds are also empaths. It is also possible that, once you start tapping into your psychic gifts, you become aware of others. As you begin to become attuned to the spiritual dimension, many other gifts of sight may develop. So there is no need to limit what you are capable of experiencing!

AURA READERS AND PAST LIFE READERS:

You might be an aura and past life reader if you checked "yes" in the Exceptional Questionnaire to any of the following questions: #2, 5, 8, 19, 23, 30

All of us are spirits in a human physical body. The body contains a partial piece of our soul and the other remains part of the non-physical world. The aura is the energy field around the body. Those that can read auras can actually see them, although they remain pretty invisible to most. You can actually feel them. Take your hand and extend it outward. Slowly bring it closer to the body. As you approach the body, close your eyes and allow your hands to move slowly, feeling for any change in energy. When you have touched your body you know that you have gone too far. You may have a tingling sensation as you feel the auric field. Those with the ability to see auras can actually see the field that surrounds the body. The auric field may have one or many colors. They can determine if it looks vibrant or if there is some stagnant energy and/or brown color. It is a way of looking at the body using your third eye. Your actual eyes may be somewhat soft as you look at the body. It takes some practice, but you might find that over time you can see the aura.

Seeing past lives is something that may develop as you look at the auric field. You may begin to sense a different time period with accompanying wardrobe. It sometimes looks like a fleeting moment but one that you can begin to recognize. It correlates with aura reading because it is developed with the third eye chakra. Learning to read past lives is valuable for connecting emotional blocks with current time reality. There are therapists that specialize in doing past live regression through hypnosis.

I had a client who was at a training seminar at the Omega Institute in Rhinebeck, New York. Although she didn't know anyone before the training, she felt a strong urge to attend this workshop on polarity healing. She was a massage therapist and thought it would help to expand her practice. When they broke for lunch the first day, she ended up connecting with a group of four women. As they were walking into the dining hall, she suddenly looked down and realized that she was wearing a nun's habit. Looking at the other women, she realized that they were all dressed similarly and that they were part of the same convent. It struck her how incredible it was that they were together at this workshop but also that they had been together in another lifetime. All four of these women had also been suffering under the same Mother Superior, who made their lives miserable. She started to remember how it felt in that lifetime to serve under someone who was so critical. The Mother Superior was constantly reprimanding her about her work. She started to connect through her intuition that this same woman was in fact one of her present co-workers at her current day job. This was one of the factors that made her work environment so unsatisfying. This woman was constantly in her face, criticizing her work despite not being her boss. As we started to process the lesson of that lifetime and how it affected her present-day reality, she realized that the Mother Superior was extremely jealous of her beauty. Despite her success in the convent, this Mother Superior resented all of her underlings and made all of their lives miserable. She realized that it wasn't personal or a reflection of her work but rather that it was the pettiness of this woman who made her life difficult. As she began to process this, she realized that she was empowering this woman at work for no reason. She didn't have any authority to be critical and it was time for my client to step into her power and stop looking for approval. Once she made that connection, this woman was no longer able to bother her at work and she found herself feeling much better. This is an example how clarifying things from a past life can free emotions for present time.

DOWSERS:

You might be a dowser if you checked "yes" in the Exceptional Questionnaire to any of the following questions: #15, 25, 27, 30

Dowsing is the ability to find water in the ground using a rod or a pendulum. People who have this talent are a very specialized lot. They take a rod or pendulum and walk over land looking for slight movements that indicate that water is below. When I lived in Vermont, dowsers were very important when people were interested in purchasing land. As you can imagine, a stream of water is important when considering any piece of property, providing water for drinking and the fields. I went out once and watched a professional dowser at work. He was a young, bearded fellow in his twenties and was dressed in cargo shorts with boots. He carried a case with several specialized kinds of dowsing rods for various environments. He picked out two, placing one in his pocket and carrying the other in his hand. We walked for about twenty minutes and he stopped suddenly. It was pretty amazing because after a few paces the dowsing rod immediately pointed at an area indicating water. He also had a shovel and started to dig. At first, I questioned his ability, but after going deeper he finally hit some moist dirt. I couldn't believe that it would happen so quickly. I know this is a specialized gift because when I tried, absolutely nothing happened. Anyone that feels this inspiration should definitely try because there are people who are happy to pay for this kind of help.

Not everyone has the ability to dowse for water. If you feel drawn to try this, I recommend reading about how to dowse. If you are able to do this, it is an ancient technique and is says more about you than the tool you use.

MEDICAL INTUITIVE:

You might be a medical intuitive if you checked "yes" in the Exceptional Questionnaire to any of the following questions: #2, 6, 8, 19, 23, 30

A medical intuitive is someone who has the ability to read the body, finding blockages and energy imbalances that cause disease or distress. A medical intuitive is able to figure out what needs to be cleared in order to find balance. Sometimes they are able to read the body through their third eye and recognize blockages in the auric field. Sometimes they can feel energy with their hands. They often recommend supplements or dietary change, as they know what is missing in someone's body chemistry. A medical intuitive can work on humans and some are able to access information on animals. These gifted healers are highly appreciated because of their extraordinary gifts and their ability to find the root causes of illness. They can clear things with their third eye without even working on the physical body. Often people in the medical field are able to begin to develop these skills as they learn about meridians and other channels of energy. As they are able to release blockages at the root level, corresponding parts of the body begin to show improvement.

We are just getting started with identifying your abilities. Please understand that this is just the beginning. As you start to connect with some of the terms used in the questionnaire, you will begin to expand your skills. Just becoming aware is a first step. It is also comforting to know that you are not alone. Others have experienced capabilities and talents similar to you.

Chapter 6 Being a Lightworker

Many of you who are drawn to understanding your supernatural gifts at this time are part of a new group of lightworkers on the planet. Those of you who want to bring about positive change are part of this group. Understanding and identifying your gifts can lead to ways that you can start to feel comfortable exploring how to utilize these abilities. Ultimately, you are learning about these talents now because there is a greater calling. Before understanding your sense of purpose, many of you were afraid of these powers, feeling that there was something that made you feel like a freak. Now you are beginning to understand that you are part of a movement of people who have very similar skills and interests. And what unifies you is the recognition that you are here to bring more light to the planet. I use the word "lightworker," but if that doesn't work for you, then you can change it. What it means to me is that you are here for a reason and that your gift is here to uplift others.

It can feel very isolating and lonely when you have psychic gifts. You can feel very much like no one understands you. However, when you begin to recognize that you are part of a larger movement, it helps to know that you are not alone.

We have all been called to live at this time because of the real growth potential. Things are accelerated on the planet and we have all decided to be here now because of the opportunity on a soul level. The energies are intensified. What used to take an entire lifetime can now be accomplished in a half a day! Seriously, we are processing through so much that this is an extraordinary opportunity for soul growth. If you look around, you can see that everyone is moving much more quickly. There is a great polarity now and it is actually being reflected all around us. Environmental global warming is also an effect of this polarity. As it is happening, we are beginning to desire more unification, as we all want to feel a greater connection to source energy. Source energy is a blend of all of our energies. It isn't just the light. It also embraces the dark forces, which are part of life. They cannot be separated.

I hope that I am not losing you here. Because, just a reminder, you are here for a reason. And your desire to learn more about your spiritual nature is leading you to realize that you are part of a larger movement. Lightworkers are needed everywhere. They are not just relegated to the fringe of society. They are needed in boardrooms and politics. Marianne Williamson, a spiritual teacher and channel, is running for President! This is not an endorsement for her; it is just stating that people who embrace the light are needed in every arena. If you see that many others with your skill sets are living active, full lives it makes it a lot less scary to embrace your own psychic spiritual skills.

When I began to realize that I was part of a movement, it made me feel less alone. It strengthened my sense of purpose and made me feel that this very particular skill was for the better good of mankind. I still realize that I can't share this with everyone. Not everyone appreciates the calling to be a lightworker and channel light onto the planet!

However, there are surprisingly a lot of us out there!

Also, the more positivity that you can experience, the more positivity you create and attract. The Law of Attraction suggests that we attract what we put out there. According to Abraham Hicks, who is channeled through Esther Hicks, the Law of Attraction is like gravity. It is law. It is undisputable. It is where like attracts like. It exists. It can be experienced when we are on a high vibration, thus attracting very positive things. When we are on a lower vibration, we can see that the things that we attract may be more undesirable. Esther and Abraham have written volumes about the Law of Attraction and it is all very helpful information. I highly recommend you check out her books and the hundreds of YouTube videos. If you get to experience one of her workshops, it's transformative.

Learning that you are part of a movement can be very empowering. It can also give you a sense of purpose, which alleviates the fear about figuring out what is going on with you. Everyone experiences fear when they are exploring things that they do not understand. As you begin to understand who you are and your skillset, you will recognize that others go through the exact same process.

Being a lightworker means keeping the awareness in your heart that you are bringing more light to the planet. It helps you to understand that your psychic sight is part of a higher plan. Learning to develop your psychic gifts gives you an opportunity for more compassion as you come to recognize that everyone is working on their problems, whether they are conscious about it or not. Your ability to see more clearly provides a reflection back to others where they are not able to see as well for themselves. It can also give tremendous insight.

Chapter 7

Consciousness

Consciousness is everything that you experience. It is the opposite of unconscious, which is a sleep state. When we are unconscious, the conscious mind is dormant and may not remember what is happening, like during anesthesia. On the other hand, as you begin to understand your psychic nature, you will come to see that you are becoming more aware of the subtle frequencies around you. Before, you were moving around without much awareness to the subtle energies. And now, you are becoming more aware of how everything affects each other. You are starting to become attuned to things that have seemed invisible before. You can feel and see things about others that perhaps they can't see. This whole process of identifying your psychic gifts is beginning to redirect your attention to a state of consciousness, where you are in a state of being awake and more aware of your surroundings. This is the beginning of your spiritual awakening.

We live in a vibrational universe where everything is part of source energy. Some like to call this "God." It really is all of the same. Every religion has a different name for it, but it is the stuff that makes up the universe. Being psychically aware means that you are starting to pay attention to that stuff. You are recognizing that it all is part of a greater whole that goes beyond each of us as individuals. It connects us. You are beginning to realize that you have an extra sense that goes beyond what we can see with our eyes. Each of you is responding to a desire to understand things at a deeper level despite the fear that it creates, or you wouldn't be here!

As you begin to develop your psychic gifts, and at this point this means being less afraid so that you can access things now, you will begin to realize that you are developing a stronger intuition. Your intuition is there to guide you. It is always there, but you can't hear it if you aren't paying attention to it. The more you listen, the stronger it gets. Life sometimes will challenge our intuition and it is often a reminder to pay attention. How often have you thought, *I should not park here, it doesn't feel right* and come back to find some kind of damage to your car? Or, *I shouldn't go down this road,* only to find a huge traffic jam? These are just slight examples of listening to your intuition. But soon, you will find that every decision you make must go through your intuition. People often ask me, "What do you think about such and such?" – and my feeling is that you honestly have your own GPS system. You know better than I do what to do! Your inner guidance is absolutely perfect and knows exactly what you need and what direction is the best for you. Honing your ability to pay attention is absolutely necessary to find the right path. My intuition has a clear light on and a light off and it has taken me years to refine it. I really work hard to not let my head make decisions based on what I want rather than what my intuition guides me to do.

Listening to your intuition often runs hand in hand but is somehow different than listening to your guidance. Guidance is being receptive to your individual Guides. Each of you has a team of non-physical helpers here while you are on the planet. They are specific to you and are here to assist you. They will never interfere unless you ask for help. They are on an on-call basis. The angelic realm is instructed not to interfere with us here, but they are always waiting to assist us. Which means it is up to us to ask for help. You can always ask your Guides for a sign. Sometimes a sign can as simple as a feather. Last week, I was looking for a new apartment with my husband and I asked for a sign about the apartment. Sure enough, it was there. I wanted to make sure that the refrigerator had glass shelves, not just wire like our last apartment. I had felt a lot of positivity about the apartment, but I asked for a sign. When I saw the shelves, it sealed the deal for me.

Another way of getting guidance is by using tools that are available. When I was growing up, I started to communicate with a pendulum. I did it as a game, not knowing that I was actually speaking to my team at an early age. The pendulum is a great tool. By sticking out your palm, you can ask the pendulum for a sign to mean yes. For me, that means the pendulum swings counter clockwise. My sign for no is when the pendulum goes directly up and down. You need to find for yourself what your signs are, as each of us is different. Clearly, the most effective way of working with a pendulum is by asking simple "yes" and "no" questions. The pendulum can't answer things on a more complex level unless you get creative. You can place the pendulum over a written statement or perhaps a job offer on paper. I don't think that I would use that tool exclusively for something so important, but if I was trying to get a spiritual read it may provide some information that could be useful. If the pendulum swings "yes" to something that I may feel is a clear "no," then that may tell me that I need more information.

Another tool for working with your guides is the tarot. Tarot cards are infused with lots of history. They are an opportunity to practice your spiritual gifts. There are simple ways of using the cards and then more complex diagrams. I have used the tarot when I am feeling confused and my intuition isn't giving me a clear indicator. There are so many different kinds of cards. I recommend going into a bookstore that sells mystical items and finding a deck that speaks to you. I will often just pick one card when I feel like I need some direction or inspiration. Our Guides are often looking for ways to get our attention and the cards can offer an easy opportunity to convey messages. Again, they will answer questions if asked. My aerobics instructor, Esmey, leaves the Unicorn

Affirmation deck out at the end of every class, and the cards are always so right on!

When we are beginning to be aware of our psychic gifts, we are often focused on others. However, the goal is really about our relationship to ourselves. We are on a journey of self-growth. Everything that happens to us is helping us progress along our own path. Our psychic spiritual journey is pushing us further into self-discovery. We are here to learn and to evolve. So although it seems terrifying to have psychic intuition, it is actually a door into the soul. When you start to become aware, it leads you forward. This actually helps to make life more meaningful and to deepen relationships. When relationships fall away, we are making space for things to come that are more in keeping with our new level of awareness. It is a constant progression forward.

In discussing consciousness, I am going to touch further on the concept of life after death. We have all commonly held the belief that you are born and then you die. When you start to understand consciousness, you realize that the energies are timeless and that there is a continuation of life before and after death. We are here to grow and expand toward a deeper consciousness that embraces life beyond the physical body. As you start to explore your psychic connections, you will begin to recognize this life force that we all share. Consciousness takes us beyond the mind into that which is all around us. It is in a constant state of flow.

Another way of looking at it is that we are in a constant flow of life force. And this force is love. Love is the energy that connects and draws us closer to source energy. It is the highest vibration. That which is not love comes from fear. Our goal is to go beyond fear, recognizing that fear does not exist. It is all part of the mind. Learning more and more about how we see the world is an opportunity to see beyond this physical planet. It is a chance to tap into that universal connection. The more we feel it and tune into it we begin to realize that fear is just a state of mind. Learning about our spirituality is an opportunity to go beyond the mind and to address our own inner being. When we tap into that energy, we find boundless love and connection to others. Our psychic gifts are an opportunity to connect with others and help them process life, too.

Energy work is taking that understanding of the universal life force and helping it move throughout the body. Many empaths and other forms of healers learn how to use their hands as a conduit for energy. Understanding consciousness allows us the chance to feel it moving through the body. Many healers are here to help us when the blocks arise and we need guidance to move the energy through. As we do that, it correlates on the physical plane, making us feel better. Energy work can be powerful. Those of you that feel things with your hands and also have access to that universal consciousness can help others tremendously. Have you ever experienced a massage with someone that seemed to know just where to go in the body to relieve stress?

Reiki is the Japanese form of healing, where trained healers access universal energy by using their hands.

"Rei" is the Japanese word for "universal life" and "Ki" means energy. Employing this technique, trained healers transfer universal energy through their palms, which encourages emotional and physical healing. This is just another way to access consciousness, or life force, and create a healing opportunity. I encourage you to experience a session and feel the power of something that is invisible to the eye but is so profound to the body. Reiki sessions are able to move through energy blocks and give an overall sense of well being.

Recognizing the many facets of consciousness helps us to understand our actions and those around us. Being able to be psychically in tune with others is another way of tapping into that energy. The more we explore this energy, the more it begins to take on a greater role in our perceptions. Instead of feeling like it is a fleeting and a terrifying experience, we begin to understand that it is just another way of reading the landscape.

Chapter 8

Clearing

As I stated earlier, we live in a vibrational universe. Everything around us is made up of energy. When we start tapping into the psychic spiritual dimension, we are beginning to touch a lot of different kinds of energies. One of the most important steps in starting to explore your own psychic nature is beginning to understand not only who you are but also who you are not. It is very easy to pick up thought forms and other kinds of energies from others without even being aware.

When I went to graduate school to get my Master of Education in Counseling, they advise that each student should enroll in therapy. The reason for this is that as you are working with many different kinds of clients, things may get triggered that you haven't realized. For example, if you have issues with your mom and your client starts talking about their difficulty communicating with their own mom, you may not be able to stay objective and see their issues clearly. You may bring up something that has to do with your own problems and not your clients', and it can get very messy. Also, when you get home that night, you may be feeling frustrated and angry and not completely understand the source of that frustration. It could be that you are carrying around your client's issues. In the same way, as you start working with psychic energy, it may be helpful for you to do either some counseling work or some healing work with a trained professional. This way you can start to be clearer as you explore your own issues, which will help you retain your clarity.

Working on yourself is important because learning to clear your own energies is a very important step when working and seeing the subtler energies. It allows you the opportunity to be objective. When you are starting to pick up things from others, you need to be able to know the difference between what is "you" and what is "them." If you are starting to get information that is really meant for another, you may not know that if you do not understand your own stuff.

For example, if you are beginning to pick up someone's fear about flying and being airborne and you are about to take a trip, it's important to realize that those fears do not belong to you. You love to travel and the excitement of packing your bags and going to the airport ready for the next adventure. But if you are starting to pack your bags and a completely irrational fear pops into your head about getting on the plane, it may be someone else's fear that you have absorbed inadvertently. This is why it is so important to understand what is yours. You can make a checklist: "No, I am not afraid of travel. This must belong to someone else. What am I picking up?"

One important process, and one I personally have to remind myself often to do, is grounding. This is a technique that means connecting with the Earth. It is a conscious decision to connect with the ground and become firmly anchored into your body. Incorporating a daily grounding ritual is a great idea to do before you leave your house each day. It means being grounded while you are driving and being grounded as you are walking down the street. It means that you are fully present in your body and feeling connected. Often I notice that things happen to me when I am not grounded. I make mistakes, bump into people, lose stuff, and don't have access to my Guides. I particularly notice that my channeling isn't as strong if I am not grounded. We need to be anchored in our bodies to handle all of the energies! Things get distorted when I am not grounded. If you find that this is a difficult concept to incorporate, take a walk outside and plant your feet on the grass. Feel the Earth's connection. Take a deep breath. I once read an article that recommended never wearing shoes so that we stayed grounded throughout the day. That would be difficult to maintain during the cold weather – but I appreciated the dedication to the importance of grounding as a tool.

It is also important to learn how to clear energies. Smudging is a practice where you take white sage and burn the leaves. Sage is an herb known for its healing and cleansing powers dating back to the American Indians. As you do this and walk around your home or office, imagine all of the discarded unnecessary energies being released. I often start with an intention before I burn the leaves. I ask that all negativity depart and that only good come to each and everyone. And as I walk around, I take a feather and blow the smoke into all directions and visualize the debris evaporating. leaving a very clean space.

A few years ago, I was walking down the street in Venice, California with two friends. A woman approached us asking if we wanted some Palo Santo. She looked like a South American medicine woman and was dressed in orange. I swear she came out of nowhere. My friends were also spiritually open, and we were all engaged instantly with this mysterious woman. She explained that her Palo Santo came from wild trees that were felled in the forests of Peru and that it was cut from very special branches and was to be used for cleansing, like sage. She said that it was a sacred wood and had medicinal properties. We were apprehensive but were willing to give it a try. I bought a few sticks for a few dollars. She said that if we wanted more that she hung out at the Whole Foods parking lot, which was ahead down the road. I went home that night to try it. It was the most incredible experience. I felt immediately uplifted after burning just a little. My dog and I sat on the couch together blissed out for a good half hour just enjoying the aroma, which was quite strong. I suggest keeping your doors and windows open. I have continued to use Palo Santo regularly in my home because of its incredible attributes. However, as many times as I have returned to Whole Foods, I never found that woman again. Her Palo Santo was the most magical that I have ever tried.

As you start to use these cleansing techniques in your home, you will begin to start to notice when the energies become stagnant. You will start to desire the lighter energies and to feel things clear from your space. You will know that the space needs cleansing. You can also smudge your friends, family, and pets. My husband just stands and asks me to smudge his aura. It really feels great. You will begin to notice if you are holding onto some negativity and start to know when it is time to smudge. It's a wonderful practice to incorporate, especially as you start to become more aware of your psychic skills.

It is also important to learn to create boundaries with family and friends. As you become more attuned to your own frequency, you will realize that you can't be receptive to others if you are not well cared for yourself. This means saying "no" at times because you don't have the reserve of energy to take on more than you can. It also means that you might not have the emotional bandwidth to take on someone else's issues. Being more sensitive vibrationally means that you need to learn to take time to decompress. It may be that smudging can revitalize your energy, but you also may need to rest. Learning how to process all of these energies takes some time. It is a great idea to reach out to a professional and get some help if you are starting to feel overwhelmed by the energies. Each of us is burning through so much on the planet at this time. This is a great time to join a group or get involved with a healing professional to learn how to process and release what is going on.

Sea salt baths are one of my favorite ways to cleanse at the end of a long day. I personally love Celtic sea salt and find it very soothing. It is relaxing and it also cleanses the aura. I have used sea salts with my children. Kids pick up so much from others because they are so receptive. They pick up discarded energies on the playground and in school. Taking a sea salt bath is a great opportunity for spiritual cleansing and unwinding after a long day.

It is also important to drink water. Water helps move the energy around. You need to drink way more than you think you do. As you work with the higher frequencies, water helps cleanse and process the energies coming in.

Thought forms are manifestations of concentrated thought. Some of you are able to pick up on these from others. It is a way of sensing or hearing what people are thinking. It is not based on reality. It is actually a thought that gains momentum and has some intensity about it. It is important to do the grounding and clearing work so that you are able to see if you are absorbing others' thought forms. Again, these are not based on reality but in fact take on momentum as others continue to feed them with continued attention. We are often influenced by thought forms, which we are not even aware we have absorbed. It is very easy to find thought forms becoming attached while getting on the subway, or a train or airplane or any contained vessel. This is something that my Guides often remind me because they are invisible and difficult to detect. So, if you are feeling suddenly preoccupied by something that doesn't connect with you, it is a perfect time to try one of the aforementioned forms of cleansing.

Chapter 9
Protection

We talked about learning how to clear our energies in the last chapter. Now we are going to be talking about the concept of protection and what this means. Again, we are now beginning to recognize that we are able to perceive much more subtler frequencies and their effect on us. As a result, we need to be much more aware of creating a positive environment as we walk among the masses. I am not suggesting that we are above others, but rather because of our sensitivity we need to be more careful out in the world. We need to learn how to protect ourselves and there are some great tools.

I first learned about Silva Mind Control many years ago. Silva Mind Control is a program developed by Jose Silva intended to increase an individual's abilities and productivity. The counselor, who introduced me to the psychic, shared some of the tools that she learned doing a Silva seminar. She taught me two really great tools that I continue to use to this day. I never took the classes, but

I know how effective these tools are because they are part of my everyday staple. I use them when I am driving, I use them when I am walking somewhere unfamiliar, I use them when I am surrounded by lots of people and there is chaos. The first tool is conjuring up "White Light." I surround myself with an imagined white light. I feel the light and wait until it seems firmly in place. This means that I am creating a protective shield around myself and I feel safer and not as vulnerable to the forces around me. I love white light. I also use it when I am thinking about my loved ones as they go about the world. Instead of worrying and projecting that negative energy, I surround my family and loved ones in a tube of white light as they go throughout the day. It clears everything for me.

Another tool that she taught me was the mirror technique. Living in New York City, there are a lot of wacky people who approach you on the street or subway. If someone is just flat out staring at me and giving me a bad feeling, I see myself surrounded in a mirrored box. This acts like a shield by bouncing their energy back to them and then they leave me alone. It is incredibly effective in turning the energy around back to the source.

Similar to using the white light, I also call on the Gold Light. It is a different kind of energy. As opposed to shielding and creating a force field like the white light, gold light is a calmer, more peaceful energy. It feels more like a cocoon. I call on the Gold Light when it seems we need some uplifting. If my kids were arguing or traffic is congested, calling on the Gold Light can help align the energies and make things go more smoothly.

Sometimes when you are aware that your energy may not be as strong and you are going out into the world, you can create a shield of protection. This may be different for each of us and I encourage you to see what inspires you. If I am feeling low energy and need to go out, I imagine a large shield protecting me. In my shield, I have different totems or spirit animals on the front. I imagine that this large shield has superpowers and is able to keep all negativity from entering my energy field. I like using gold as the base, but other colors can be useful as well. Imagine a blank canvas and fill it however you would like, knowing that the intention is to protect your space. When your intent is to create protection, the shield will serve that purpose.

Chapter 10

A Practice of Gratitude

One way of keeping us on a high vibration is the practice of gratitude. Gratitude, or appreciation, is an opportunity to tell the universe all of the wonderful things that we are happy about. When we do this, it absolutely helps us feel our most positive selves. Researchers have found that groups of participants who kept journals and wrote down five things that they were grateful about were twenty-five percent happier than a group that wrote down things they were upset about or a neutral group who were not told whether to write down happy or negative circumstances. They reported fewer health complaints and exercised about 1.5 hours more during the week than the other groups. (Collective-Evolution.com).

A practice of gratitude means taking out a few minutes each day to acknowledge all of the things in our lives that we appreciate by writing them down. Many choose to have a gratitude journal that is meant specifically for keeping track on a daily basis. Starting the day writing a list of things to appreciate raises our vibration so that we can go forward into the day on a very high note. As we have discussed, the power of the law of attraction means that when we are on a higher vibration, we attract more positive circumstances.

The practice of gratitude also helps shift the circumstances when we are actually having a bad day and things aren't going our way. When you take a step back to pause and write down the things that you are feeling grateful for at that minute, you pivot away from the negativity, which allows some positive aspects to come forth.

As highly sensitive beings attuned to the more subtle frequencies, we need to be able to create positivity when we get overwhelmed with negative energies. The practice of gratitude on a daily basis really anchors us in a positive direction. It helps us get some distance from when we are overwhelmed by negative circumstances. It especially helps if we find that we are unconsciously holding on to energies that aren't ours. As we start to feel the shift by practicing gratitude, we are more able to release that which doesn't really belong to us.

As we discussed earlier, our role as a lightworker means that we are channeling light to the planet at this very important time of ascension. When we practice gratitude, it helps us stay more firmly rooted in a positive perspective. It is incredibly effective, and it builds momentum with continued practice. Momentum about positive things creates more positive things. When you are feeling that positive vibe it means that you can more easily process negative emotion. This is especially true when you are absorbing things from others and may not realize what it is going on. The practice of gratitude means that you are more resistant to the negative energies of others. It is just harder to negatively influence a person anchored in positivity.

Chapter 11

The Importance of a Meditation Practice

Meditation is an often-complex experience with different meanings for each individual. As we have discovered our psychic, spiritual self, it is important to discuss the purpose of meditation. We need to explore why it is important, what it offers each of us, and why a regular daily meditation practice is essential.

Meditation can be practiced in many forms. There really is not one correct way to meditate. Some people are more comfortable using sounds, some are more comfortable using a mantra, and others enjoy using visual imagery as a launching point for meditation. The "how" is not important as each person finds ways that work for them. What is important is that it becomes incorporated into a daily routine and practiced on a regular basis.

One reason that we meditate is that it is a time of allowing. It differs from sleep in that there is a conscious expansion that occurs and in those moments of meditation there is a moment of clarity. As we on Earth are living in a physical experience, meditation is a time that allows our soul to make contact by quieting the mind. Often, we confuse our thoughts with reality. We believe that the thoughts coming from our mind are truth. In moments of clarity during meditation, there is an allowing where the soul has an opportunity to be heard. And in those moments, we understand that we are beings beyond physical reality. There really is no goal in meditation and to approach it as such often is confusing. It is a quieting for no other purpose other than to sense that deep connection beyond thoughts and everyday reality. And in doing so, in creating a practice that allows a meditation time each day, it creates an opportunity for realignment. Aligning with source is the most important activity each day because it elevates us beyond our everyday understanding and brings with it knowledge of who we are and why we are here. And in knowing that, we will find peace. This peace brings about clarity and clarity helps us to feel more joy. And it is through joy that we begin to feel a true deep connection. It is from this deep connection that we create the most meaningful relationships.

Meditation does bring in positive benefits in other ways as well. We no longer react to everyday drama because we have that moment to pause and step back. Meditation is restorative and it is a practice that deepens each time we practice. It takes less time to get into that space of allowing the more frequently we do it. Not that it needs to happen for hours on end – just fifteen to twenty minutes each day can be life changing. The physical benefits are real. The result of that realigning lowers blood pressure because it is a moment of letting go. The deep relaxation is a result of calming the mind.

It is recommended to just create the time for practice without expectation. It is not an "efforted" activity. Sometimes it takes time to get into a rhythm and to feel a difference. After practicing for several weeks, it is possible to notice slight changes. Again, this is quite individual to each person. It's not a competition! What is important is that over time, you will begin to feel the benefits. You might notice that you are slower to react to something or that you are starting to feel calmer. These are some of the benefits. For me, the practice of meditation gives me a clearer mind and a stronger sense of who I am so that I can let go of drama that does not belong to me. I feel a sense of calm that stays with me throughout the day.

Dr. Herbert Benson, of Harvard University can be credited for making meditation mainstream in the sixties and seventies by renaming it the "Relaxation Response." It was there that he began to study the real effects of meditation on hypertension and stress. His studies showed that meditation promotes better health, especially in individuals with hypertension. People who meditate regularly enjoy increased well being, lower stress levels, reduced blood pressure levels and resting heart rate.

Dr. Benson worked with the Maharishi Mahesh Yogi, who started TM, a mantra meditation. This is how I got started. I read that Dr. Benson recommended using a mantra, like the word "one," to keep the brain occupied while concentrating on deep breathing. I had discovered a list of mantras printed in the paper, and found one that I liked. For those that do the TM program, you have a specialized guide who gives you a word and teaches you the process as well as checking in to make sure that you are on track. The David Lynch foundation, based on TM, is an incredible organization and provides lots of freebies for students, prisoners, and veterans. My husband loved the process of TM and felt more comfortable with a guide. For me, I was in college when I started, and it was just the easiest and cheapest way to learn. I would take the recommended twenty minutes and find a quiet place to sit. Twice a day I would go to my special spot and close my eyes. Using the mantra became quite comfortable and would signal to my body that we were going into a deeper state. I would focus on the mantra and when I noticed my mind drifting, I would gently bring it back to the mantra. I soon loved the time when I would not be thinking. It gave me some distance from my mind, which had positive effects after the meditation was over. I started to realize that my mind could just keep going in circles, and having some ability to get off that cycle helped me. I still meditate with the same mantra. It has given me an inner core of strength, building on all of those years with the same mantra. Sometimes I experience a very deep meditation, while others feel lighter. If I am extremely distracted, it can be harder to stay focused. At other times I find that I need to recharge, and meditating is the only way for me to go inside and feel replenished. It takes a little time to get used to it, and I recommend trying to find the same time each day for your regular practice. This way your body knows what to expect and it automatically prepares for the meditative state.

For those of you with a more auditory sensibility, focusing on a sound in the same way I use the mantra can be very effective. I have a friend who loves the sound of her air conditioner! You could use a metronome or find some kind of sound that you find comforting. You want to pick a sound that is constant and unwavering. It is the same practice; every time you find your mind wandering, go back to the sound that is a constant. Let that guide you as you quiet the mind and go deeper.

I recommend starting with a mantra meditation because it is the easiest and least complicated to get results. I am going to give you a detailed description so that you can try this yourself.

MANTRA MEDITATION

1. Choose a quiet location and find a comfortable seat. I start cross-legged on the floor, but you may prefer a chair. It is important not to lie down because you may end up falling asleep and you do want to stay alert. Get comfortable.

2. Pick a mantra. You can choose the word OM, which means peace. Or you can use the word ONE. Make it simple.
3. I use the timer on my phone. I find the softest ring tone so that it won't be jarring, alerting me abruptly. There is one that sounds like soft rain called SILK.
4. Set it for five, ten, fifteen, or twenty minutes. I would start slow and build up, as you get more comfortable.
5. Close your eyes.
6. Start becoming aware of your breath. You will begin to notice your inhaling and exhaling.
7. Start repeating the mantra over and over again.
8. You will start to notice sounds or thoughts wanting your attention. Whenever you notice your mind drifting to what is distracting you, gently bring it back to the mantra. Let your mantra be your anchor. It is there to support you and to give your mind something to hold on to. Keep bringing your attention back to the mantra.
9. You can use your breath to work with the mantra. Deep breathe in and out as you say the mantra.
10. When you notice that your time is up or your alarm has signaled that the time is over, give yourself some time to come back into your body. Do not rush to stand up. Feel your hands and your

legs. Take some very deep breaths. Wait until you feel grounded before getting up.

11. If you are looking for messages from your guides, this is a good time to be receptive, as your mind is relaxed. You may want to keep your journal nearby so that you can write down anything that comes to mind.
12. If you can repeat this at the same time each day, your body will begin to expect the process and you will move into the meditation more easily. Make a decision to do if for a week and watch for any changes during the day. Are you able to react to things more slowly because you feel a sense of calm throughout the day? Pay attention. As you begin to see some benefits, it will motivate you to continue your practice.

For those of you that find the mantra or sound meditation to be difficult, there are some amazing apps now that give lots of guidance throughout the process. You can Google some available apps and find one that you feel connected to that works with your pocketbook.

Some find that sitting is too difficult. Some say that walking is their preferred route for meditation. This works as long as your intention is for meditation and not just chatting on the phone. Others like painting as a form of meditation. As long as you are committed to a daily practice, and recognize that the space is held for the purpose of realigning on a deeper basis, you can find what works best.

I wanted to share a guided meditation that I received from my Guides. It was an extremely vivid experience and I knew it wasn't a dream. I often awake to lessons from my Guides and I try and write it down so I don't forget. The beauty of a guided meditation is that you don't have to do any work and can just follow along. You may wish to record the meditation so that you can listen later. This way you can enjoy the experience without having to continually check the next steps.

MEDITATION TO GET IN TOUCH WITH YOUR PSYCHIC GIFTS:

1. Begin by getting comfortable in a seated position.
2. Take some deep breaths and try and let go of any stagnant energy.
3. We will begin by doing some grounding. Feel the energy from your spine, or root chakra, go all the way into the core of the Earth. Take some deep breaths here, feeling a sense of connection and some light. You may actually feel the Earth and she may have a message for you. Listen to hear what she is saying. As you feel the roots going into the core, feel that deep sense of connection. Feel as though nothing can take you out of position. Feel as though you are completely grounded and connected to the Earth's core. You may feel a color. Breathe it in and out, releasing anything that feels that it is no longer of use. Ask if you are holding onto anything that is no longer serving you. Be aware if you are holding onto something

that doesn't belong to you. Have you picked up energies from another? Ask! If you are aware that you are holding on to something that isn't yours, take some deep breaths and send it out with your breath. Become aware if there are other energies that you are holding onto at this time and release anything that is not yours or no longer serves you.

4. As you let go, bring your energy up into your second chakra, which is your sexual center. Feel the energy here and ask the same questions. What am I holding on to that is no longer serving me? Am I holding on to another's energies? Is there anything there that I can release at this time? Use your breath to clear the energy. If it helps to breathe out a color and then breathe in a color, use your breath to do so. This is your journey and your moment to let go of anything that doesn't serve you. Keep checking to make sure that you are feeling that connection to the Earth's energy.
5. Next, bring your breath up to the will center, or third chakra, located in your belly. Feel the energies using your breath. Is there anything that you are holding onto at this time? Are you aware of anyone else's energies in there that no longer belong? Take some time and feel the breath here so that you are comfortable with what you are experiencing. Feel that sense of connection to the Earth anchoring your experience. When you

are feeling that the energy is clear, bring in some golden light and feel a sense of calm.

6. When you are ready, bring your breath up to your heart center, or fourth chakra. It is the area around your heart. Check out what's going on. Do you feel the need for a color? Use your breath to bring in anything that you think will soothe it. Are you aware of any energy that doesn't belong to you? Are you feeling anything that is no longer serving you? Are there any emotions that you feel need to be released? Take your time.
7. When you are ready bring your breath up into your throat chakra; this is the area in your throat that holds your communication center or fifth chakra. Feel the energy. Make sure that you can still feel the connection with the Earth. Take slow deep breaths and feel the energy climb back up into this center. Check out what's going on. Do you feel that it needs some color? Do you sense that you are holding on to energy from another? Can you feel that you are holding on to anything that you need to release? This is a great time to release anything that is no longer serving you using your breath.
8. When you feel that the energy has been cleared and is balanced, move your breath up into your third eye. This is the area between your two eyes above the brow in your forehead. This is your spiritual sight. This is where you have access to the

other dimensions. This is where you may begin to recognize that you have some ability to see. Before we talk about abilities, we want you to clear this sixth chakra. Again, using your breath, feel if there is anything that you are holding onto here. Are you experiencing anything that isn't yours? Are you feeling energy that no longer serves you? Perhaps you are aware of an event that you are beginning to remember that no longer is useful for you now. Or perhaps there is some learning here that you want to remember. Using your breath, exhale anything that you no longer need. Feel a light connection. Feel that energy begin to circulate and to feel open.

9. When it feels right, take that energy and breathe out the top of your head. This is the crown chakra, or the seventh chakra. Feel it opening and connecting into the universe. Feel the energy from the Earth's core all of the way up to the top of your head. Again, pay particular attention to the energies here. Are you holding onto anything that isn't yours? Can you feel anything that is stagnant and needs to be released? Can you feel that you are holding on to something that isn't yours? It may be surprising to find something here that doesn't belong to you.
10. Sit here for a moment feeling the energies moving through the core of the Earth out to the top

of your head. Feel a gold light connecting these centers. Feel your energy, strong and powerful.

11. And now, take your breath to the area above your crown. This is the eighth chakra and connects you to the heavens. It feels so amazing to have this light go from the Earth to the heavens. If you feel that something is being held that isn't yours, ask for it to be released. Feel the connection to source. Feel the connection to your inner being. This is a powerful experience and one that you can draw on throughout the day.
12. Now, that you are feeling connected, grounded and inspired, ask yourself about your own special gifts. What are you here for? What special psychic gifts are yours? Can you feel them now? Are you getting any messages? If not, please do not be alarmed. They may come later when you are not aware. But, now, when you are feeling this connection to your inner being, is a great time to receive guidance. Sit quietly and let it come. Feel your breath as it guides you. And feel that part of you that is unique to your own energy. Feel that connection to the Earth and Sky. Take notice of anything that comes into your mind. Use any color that calls for attention. Use the colors to help uplift your energy if you feel the need.
13. After you sit with this for a while, bring your awareness back to your breath. Feel your body and the breath going in and out. Feel yourself be-

coming more aware of your body. Ask yourself if there is anything that you need to remember before you awaken from this meditation so that you don't forget. Know that you can come back here at any time. This is your sacred temple. Right now. Right here. This is your special space. When you start to become aware of sounds and smells around you, you can slowly open your eyes.

14. And just like that, you are back. This is a good time to write down anything that you have learned or became aware of during the meditation. Writing what you have experienced allows you the opportunity to connect and make it more active in your consciousness. Take some deep breaths to ground your energy after you have allowed time for receiving messages. Feel your body and acknowledge what you just experienced. You can try this again and again if you feel inspired to do so. It is very important not to force anything. If you don't feel anything at this time, that is perfect, too. Sometimes awareness comes when you least expect it. Each time you meditate, you are making shifts. It will come.

ANOTHER GUIDED MEDITATION: COLOR MEDITATION

This is a meditation that my Guides taught me at night. It was like a dream, but I could remember every detail. I knew that my Guides were talking to me and I was aware of the experience of the meditation. I knew when I awoke to write this down. So here it is for you.

When you call upon colors you are bringing a frequency into your energy field that lifts and affects each of you in different ways. Although I spoke to you earlier in the book about the meanings of different colors, they really could have different interpretations for each of you. But let's start talking about using colors in meditation understanding that they bring forth specific vibrations.

1. I will start by guiding you to prepare for being receptive to this experience. I ask that you get into a comfortable position. And starting from the crown chakra, feel the energy reach into the sky, bringing golden light into the crown of the head and bringing it all the way down the spine – all of the way, piercing into the Earth and deep down into the Earth's core. As you feel that energy, you can feel that golden light like a beam from heaven into the Earth's core, aligning your energy as it travels through your chakras. This allows a clearing and grounding of sorts, as we get ready for the color meditation.
2. Now, as you are feeling that sense of connection and feeling a sense of calm, I ask you to bring your attention to the third eye center, which is in the center of the forehead. For those new to this concept, the third eye opens to the spiritual center and allows one to see beyond the physical world into the beyond. It is here, with eyes closed, that I

want you to begin your color meditation. Instead of using a mantra, I ask that you bring forth a color that is inspiring to you. It may be magenta, or green, or orange. It can be a variety of colors from the rainbow. Don't analyze what it means or what you "should" bring forth. See what color inspires you right now and let it fill up your third eye. Feel the color take shape and pour into the center as it begins to vibrate and shimmer. Sit with this for a while and if it seems appropriate, bring forth another color. See if you feel attracted to bringing in another color or whether you want to continue with what was there. Just allow the new or continued color to fill up your mind and experience the sensation that it brings. This can last for as long or as short a time as you wish. If you feel drawn to bring in another color, do. Keep doing this for as long as you wish. If you feel the need for a new color, bring another color into the third eye. Use your breath to flame the color, making it deeper and more robust. If you love this color, let it stay for a while and bask in its light.

3. After you feel like you have achieved clarity and relaxation or a feeling of alignment, bring your attention back into your breath. Slowly move your hands and feet as you bring your consciousness into your body. And then when you are ready, you can open your eyes. If you experience anything that you want to remember, add it to your journal so that you will remember it later.

Chapter 12
Modern Day Tools

Now that we have our meditation practice in place, there are so many wonderful tools available to help you on your journey. Many of these tools have been around throughout history and are still available now. Some of them are new. This is actually my favorite section, as I use these tools every single day to help uplift me as well as cleanse my energy.

Perhaps many of you have seen a new resurgence in crystals. People are wearing them more and stores are popping up everywhere. Crystals have been around since the time of Atlantis and long before. They elevate energy and each one comes with a very special code specifically designed to work with you and help you on your journey. People use them in meditation, as jewelry, in the home as decorations, and in healing grids.

If crystals are new for you, I suggest you start with a basic quartz crystal. They are very reasonably priced and the easiest to use. If I were to only have one crystal at my disposal, it would be quartz. They come in a variety of sizes and you can get one small enough to put in your pocket or one large enough to have on your nightstand or desk. The beauty of quartz is that they are very easy to clean and simple to use.

You can buy a quartz crystal in a crystal store, but there are lots of beautiful stones available now on Etsy and other sites as well. You can actually buy crystals on Amazon. I have done that, but I warn against it, as the quality is not always as good. I once made the mistake of buying a crystal on a random Instagram site, only to find out that it came from China. I was attracted to the picture, which was an unusual orange. In person it was really just a quartz crystal with artificial color added and it was completely different than the one in the picture.

When buying a crystal, choose something that feels good. Find a crystal that you are attracted to. By that, I mean one that you keep going back to, one that you want to hold and can't seem to put down. Your crystal will help you find it. You will know it's right, because you won't want to leave it in the store. If you are feeling uncertain, you can always ask for help by the storeowner – but I recommend that you absolutely trust your intuition here. Your Guides will be showing you the way. If not, just find one that you like based on its appearance alone. That is a great way to start.

A good way to start with a quartz crystal is by holding it in your hand. Spend some time looking at the little nooks and crannies inside. Usually there is a pointed end and a bottom that is visible. The tip directs the energy outwards. When you are holding the crystal, you may want to close your eyes and feel the energy. Can you feel any kind of vibration? Does it feel good? Are you feeling any kind of energy block in your body? Put the crystal on the block and point outwards. It can help release energy that is no longer serving you. It can clear your auric fields.

Because of their ability to absorb energy, crystals need to be cleansed. Clear quartz crystals can be cleansed differently than colored crystals, like amethyst. Because quartz doesn't have any color, it can be exposed to direct sunlight. Any crystal with color will fade under direct sunlight. The sun actually clears the energy effectively in quartz. Another way to clear quartz is by putting it in a sea salt bath. As with colored crystals, sea salt is not recommended because it will cause the color to fade. Just fill a bowl with water and add some sea salt. You can also bathe in sea salt with the crystals. This method will really cleanse your aura and clean your crystals at the same time. If you have a garden, you can put your crystal in the dirt. The Earth energy is a great way to recharge your crystal. Moonlight is also a way of cleansing crystals. It has no harmful effect on crystals with color, so it is a safe way to recharge them all. You can make a ritual by bringing out the crystals during a full moon. You can let your crystals recharge during the moonlight while also having a sacred full moon meditation. The ancients believe that a full moon is a time of maximizing the energy and releasing that which has been building expanding one's potential.

Smudging sage and Palo Santo is also an effective cleanser and safe for all crystals including those with color like amethyst or citrine. Take your Palo Santo stick or sage bundle and light it carefully. You can just bathe the crystal in the smoke plume to clean it from any old, stale energy while bringing your crystal back into alignment. There are so many beautiful colored crystals available today and all of them require some form of clearing after use.

I hold crystals when I sleep, when I meditate, when I cleanse my aura, and when I want to create positive energy in my home. Crystals create a loving, positive vibe and really help those that are beginning to absorb negativity from others. Working with crystals brings lots of light into the home or office.

Although all crystals are recommended for highly sensitive people, amethyst is really helpful for empaths. It is grounding and protective as well as helping release energies that no longer serve. Smudging, bathing in moonlight or soaking in a bath with sage leaves can cleanse Crystals. See what draws you in. Once you start attuning to your crystals, they will let you know when they need to be cleansed. Until then, make it part of your routine.

Essential oils are another wonderful tool promoting well-being and decreasing stress. Plant-based healing has been recommended since the beginning of time. These oils have so many different therapeutic values. It is important to use pure organic essential oils to get the highest quality and vibration. Higher quality oils are more effective because they carry the most pure form of the plant. People can use oils for their aromatic properties as well as other benefits when absorbed by the skin or taken internally. In ancient times, the Egyptians and the Romans used oils for bathing, relaxing, cooking, and as a perfume. You can use the oils before meditation by rubbing on your third eye or on the top of your head, in a bath, or in a diffuser.

There are three oils that I would recommend if you were just getting started. I would recommend lavender immediately. Lavender is probably the most frequently recognized for its healing benefits. It calms anxiety and helps ease feelings of stress and anxiety. I once had an MRI where I was extremely tense, and the technician put a drop on my cloth robe. It really helped me relax. Despite my history of working with oils, I was surprised by how quickly and effectively the lavender oil helped me relax. The delicious aroma transported me to a much happier place.

Another of my favorites is frankincense, which promotes feelings of peace, relaxation, and overall wellness. It helps with reducing chronic pain and inflammation and boosting immunity. Frankincense is also recommended for treating issues with the skin from combatting dryness to smoothing wrinkles. It also smells great when added to a diffuser.

The third oil that I would recommend would be lemon. Lemon has multiple benefits and uses. It is a cleansing agent that purifies the air and is also great in a diffuser. When it is diffused, it is uplifting and energizing, improving mood. It provides cleansing and digestive benefits and supports a healthy respiratory function.

As I have been saying throughout this book, begin to use your intuition. If you are feeling drawn to a certain essential oil, find out what it can do for you. Very recently I was guided to buy an essential oil that I hadn't ever smelled, and I knew nothing about it. When I asked my knowledgeable friend his thoughts about the oil, he sent me a long description. It was absolutely so appropriate for what I was going through. The oil was Melissa. We had just had a fire in our apartment building and we had to move. I was feeling anxious and confused about the experience. Melissa is known for being uplifting and helping with anxiety. It really did make me feel better and lighter emotionally.

One last trick: if you don't like the way the oils smell but want to experience some of the benefits, you can always put them on the bottoms of your feet. This way they are absorbed into the body without having to go through your nose. Often if you are wearing several oils at the same time and you don't want them to compete with each other, you can try the soles of your feet and get the exact same benefits.

Another wonderful tool is using affirmations. Affirmations are a way of focusing the energy into a positive intent. If you are not happy about a certain set of circumstances, creating positive affirmations is a way of redirecting the energy. We talked earlier about making a practice of positive appreciation or gratitude. This is different because we are talking about something that we desire. Affirmations are extremely powerful. This is something that cannot be directed for another person. You can't make affirmations about someone else because each of us has free will. Affirmations are really helpful in focusing what we want to see happen. They can be used with goals ranging from improved health to creating abundance. Affirmations affect all of our self-talk. It is a way of making our internal vocabulary beneficial and recognizing the importance of positive language. Affirmations make us aware of what we intend and creates responsibility for our actions by creating more awareness about what and how we are thinking.

Another of my favorite tools is the Light-Life ring and Light-Life Acu-Vac Coil. One is a gold ring and the other looks like a gold coil. A man named Slim Spurling invented these tools and you can read more about them on his homepage, Light-Life Technology. The ring brings positive life-force energy to everything in their field. The coils act as a vacuum and are able to draw out any negative energy. These tools are amazing at cleansing the energy and bringing in positive energy. They can be used on everything from clearing crystals to giving more life energy to water. They can be used with jewelry or anything that you feel is holding negative energy. If something comes into my house that feels funky, we give it a session with the gold ring. The coil is also wonderful for drawing out anything that feels congested. I have used it on my kids, on my pets, and on anything else that doesn't resonate a high vibration. These tools are simply amazing, and I recommend reading more about them on the Light-Life home page.

Another great tool for clearing energy is the Rose Tool. I first learned about the Rose Tool with Jim Self, the teacher and creator of a course called Mastering Alchemy. You begin by being in a meditative state, relaxed and comfortable. When you notice that you are holding energy that doesn't belong to you, you can bring in a visualized rose. Imagine that the rose has no color. You can make it large or small, but it must have a stem. Point the stem towards the area that needs clearing and imagine that the energy is being drawn out into the petals of the rose. It may give the petals a color. As the energy is being drawn out, you can visualize the rose growing and expanding with all of the discarded energy. It may turn a color that symbolizes to you all of the unwanted energy. When it gets to the point where you can feel there is no more left to draw out, focus back on the rose. The rose has expanded now with all of that energy and is engorged. Imagine the rose bursting with all of the discarded energy and send it up into the Universe for clearing. Take some deep breaths and feel yourself reorienting back to your own body with your breath. Feel a sense of balance and calm.

The goal of all of these tools is to create more positivity and to help clear anything that doesn't resonate on a high level of energy. As you begin to become more attuned to your sensitivity, these levels of energy will become more apparent. You will begin to have a physical need to purge anything that doesn't resonate on a higher frequency. As you start working with the tools, they will become more comfortable. Each of you will have your own methods that work and you will find other ways to keep your energy in a positive direction. It is important to recognize that although you will become more sensitive to the energies around you, you now have tools to help release things. It doesn't mean that you can't go anywhere. Instead, you have more tools accessible so that you can interact with confidence. If you absorb something that doesn't feel aligned, you have tools to release that energy. You interacting with the world and sharing your light is what it's all about!

Chapter 13

What Now?

As you have learned about being a lightworker, now is the time for a call to action. We are part of that movement. This means that we aren't supposed to live on a mountaintop and just meditate all day long. We are here to live in the world and bring our light to others. Which means ask yourself – what am I here to bring to my current job or relationship? What are my sensitivities telling me at this time? Is there something that I need to add at work or in my family to bring greater harmony and well being? Instead of seeing yourself as two separate people, the "normal" versus the "psychic" me, think of you as two complements to one whole. This is a great time for you to recognize that there is a gift and purpose to your special skills. The planet needs you! Often, once we start the regular meditation practice, we notice that certain messages come up. After that time of quieting the mind, we are ripe for messages from our inner being and also our guides. This is a great time to open your journal and write thoughts or messages down before you forget. As I was preparing to write this book, I went back and looked at my journal. There were so many messages about writing a book! It started as something from my intuition, but it grew into desire. I have wanted to do this for a long time.

Often you get messages when it is time to move on from a relationship, job, or living situation. These messages are important to hear. The more we listen to our inner being and guidance, the stronger their messages are and the easier it is to hear them. I now know that I can access this when I need to instead of just after a meditation. My inner voice has to be included on everything I do. It is the times that I don't listen that I am reminded why I do. My inner guidance system and psychic self knows best. With journaling or writing down specific messages, you have a record of things that come your way. They may not always make sense but later when you review you may see a theme.

Regarding others, just because we are able to pick up messages about someone else doesn't give us license to tell people what to do. We don't know if they would even be receptive to our messages. It takes some finesse to figure out how to share things that come our way. If you are in a professional counseling or coaching situation, it is easier to figure out how to access these skills. However, if the guy sitting across from you is dealing with a ton of sadness and you can't ignore it, you might need to put up one of your shields. You may want to bring some crystals to work to help you clear the energies. You may choose to bring and or wear some essential oil. At least now, you get to choose whether you absorb energies or guard against them. You have more ability to choose how to interact with the environment around you.

Understanding that you have a psychic spiritual intuition means that you can be more confident in trusting what you feel. Remember that the future is not set in stone. We live in a vibrational universe where things are constantly changing. If you are becoming aware of negative things coming your way and you have that clairvoyance, you can ask your Guides to tone it back if you are getting more than you can handle. You have control over what you see. It is important to know that. I know how overwhelming it can be.

If things continue to feel overwhelming, it is important to use your grounding tools. Sometimes the energies can be intense. The Earth is realigning itself and that creates a lot of psychic stress. Take a walk in nature. Use the root chakra in a meditation. Find the rose tool and see if you are holding onto stuff that isn't yours. Take a yoga class and get really anchored in your body. Exercise! Drink lots and lots of water. Feel the Earth beneath your feet. Sometimes it means just saying "no" to a social activity because you aren't feeling centered. Listen to your body.

Your sensitivity requires paying attention. When you are feeling overwhelmed you need to listen. If you get the sense that you need to avoid something or someone, listen. I am not suggesting that you become a recluse. Rather, begin to see that you are your best advisor. You know what works best for you. No one can read you like you do. Trust yourself. If you need a little assistance, grab one of your tarot decks and pick a card. Maybe that is what you need to receive an uplifting message. Don't diffuse your sensitivities by asking for advice. You are the person that knows what is best for you.

Finding that connection to your inner being is the best anchor into your truth. Making peace with that inner being and learning to understand her/him is the best way to feel connection to joy and happiness. Our spiritual attunement often makes us aware of negative emotion, but it is there to help us learn more about what we want. Sometimes we have to sit with those feelings despite their being uncomfortable. When we connect to our inner joy, it becomes reflected in the stuff around relationships, work, home, and ourselves.

Becoming comfortable with our spiritual self adds more dimensions to our experiences. We start to see things on a deeper level. We make deeper connections with others. It expands our knowledge and connects us to a deeper sense of well being. We are able to be more present and to live in the *now*. When we are living in the present, it is the most powerful place. We are able to access our power and make the decisions that serve us the best. Learning all of these things can open so many wonderful opportunities.

Chapter 14
Dealing with Challenges

When you start to appreciate your psychic spiritual self, you realize how sensitive you are to all of the energies around you. Keeping firm boundaries is very important. You can't take on everything. You will become aware that certain events and people drain you. Family can be challenging. The word "no" can be quite empowering. It is important to trust your inner voice when it steers you clear from an event or gathering. If you are feeling overwhelmed, you may need to have some alone time or get together with a friend instead of being involved with a larger group.

We have talked so far about keeping protection from others, but it is time to talk about the spiritual energies, the light and dark forces. There is only light and love but in the absence of that can be fear and darkness.

That is why it is important to always call upon the light before doing energy work. Ask your angels to guide and protect you. Remember, they will not interfere unless you ask for their assistance. Before I do any channeling or energy work, I always call upon my angels to come and be with me and ask all negative energies to depart. I ask for only good to come to each and every one and that the work is for the highest good. I want my work to have the highest form of integrity and in doing so, I make sure to create that positive intent at the beginning of everything. Also, in calling for the highest good, I want to override my own personal ego so that the best and clearest communication is available. There are a lot of low-rent non-physical entities out there and it is not my intention to channel their energy. Just because something is a spirit doesn't mean that they have access to high-level information. It is important to be discerning. Recognize that you always want the purest forms of light to come when you are open. Asking for protection is a great way to start any communication with the non-physical or psychic energies.

People ask if they should share this knowledge with their family and friends. Often in doing so, they open themselves to scrutiny or condemnation. It seems best to share when you are feeling stable and grounded in your beliefs. As you are just becoming aware of some of your psychic abilities, you may want to wait until you are more confident. This way, if someone is disapproving, you will recognize that it is about his or her fear and not yours. If you feel that you can't contain it any longer, recognize that you don't need approval. If you know who you are, then it doesn't really matter how people react.

Often people share that they are overwhelmed. Being sensitive can open you up to lots of different energies. You may feel stuff from family, friends, and coworkers, as well as planetary energy that is in constant motion. Highly sensitive people can experience reactions to solar flares, which occur when magnetic energy builds up in the solar atmosphere, causing it to erupt. We also have a fair number of eclipses each year, which cause intensity in the energy and affect us in different ways. As you learn your own body and energy you can learn how to navigate all of this.

Feeling overwhelmed may also be a sign that you could use some assistance in the form of an acupuncture treatment, Reiki, or massage session. Bodywork is a great way to alleviate stress and remove blockages. When you are intuitive, working with a healer is a great way to learn how to be in touch with your own energies and find ways to learn how to release stagnant energy. If you don't like the physical sensation of a massage, Reiki treatments are pure energy and can feel great. Because of your sensitivities, you want to work with people who are very highly aligned to positive energies.

When you are overwhelmed, simplify. Go back to the basics. Use your grounding tools. Take a warm bath. Get in bed with a book or watch a movie on Netflix. Self-care is very important. Journal to see if you can sort out your feelings about what is going on. Hang out with friends with whom you can share what is happening.

Therapy can be very helpful at this time with a trained counselor or therapist who understands what you are going through. You may want to find a group with other intuitives for support. I will be including my contact information at the end of the book. Please reach out, as I will be putting together groups on an ongoing basis. Sometimes just knowing that others are going through the same thing can help us feel less alone and more validated. In groups, we find that others may make recommendations that may be new and valuable and it is great to have support.

Working with a past life regression therapist can help you find blocks that you may have not even known that you had. In a very protected environment, the therapist takes you deep to explore energies beyond this physical lifetime. Once the blocks are revealed, we see that they are often reflected here and now. Being able to identify their energies is a great learning tool and helps move us forward.

Whenever the blocks and obstacles arise, we need to remember that they are here to teach us. There is usually a lesson of value. Often the universe is redirecting us in a different direction. Our daily meditation practice allows us the opportunity to witness experiences without reacting. This helps alleviate the stress so that we can see more clearly during difficult times. In Chinese, the word for "crisis" is danger and opportunity. When we are more centered we can approach difficulty with a calmer mind. There is always something of value despite appearances.

Chapter 15
Conclusion

At the beginning of this book, you may have felt that your psychic sensitivity was causing you to feel crazy at times and was unexplained by popular research. Many of you came to find out if your experiences could be explained. You were overwhelmed and felt that you couldn't discuss things with your friends or family for fear of judgment and the possibility that they would confirm that you are in fact crazy!

Your anxiety levels have hit an all-time high and you have been feeling internal stress, causing headaches and digestive issues. You had a suspicion that you might have psychic tendencies, but just the thought of that kicked up fear of the unknown and terror that you might be some freak.

I want you to know my story so that you know that you are not alone. I grew up in a very traditional background and yet my experiences were so real and clear that I couldn't doubt what I felt. I want you to know how easy it is to internalize shame and insecurity when you see things that others are not seeing. Those feelings create so much doubt and really make it difficult to trust our inner knowing. When you are intuitive, trusting those feelings is the basis of everything. Feeling any kind of insecurity puts the whole system in jeopardy. Hopefully, knowing that you aren't alone has started you on a journey to trust your vision. Maybe you have also wondered if there was more than meets the eye. Your inner being has brought you here and now it's time to activate this part of you.

Exploring the concept of psychic here means understanding the energies around us on a very subtle level. It isn't about seeing terrifying events in the future. We are learning how to identify our own special skills. You actually took the Exceptional Quiz to figure out what makes you tick. *How do I interpret the universe? What subtle energies am I reading from others? What is it about me that make me Exceptional?*

Learning how to identify your own specialized skills makes them less frightening. Although each of you is unique, you see that your skillset is something that can be shared and something that you can explore. There is so much material out there if you want to pursue your abilities, because you know now that you are a lightworker. Being a lightworker means that you are part of a movement to bring light to the Earth. It means that there is purpose to your experiences as a psychic, spiritual person. Knowing that there is purpose, changes everything from feeling that you are just at the effect of wild and crazy energies to being part of a movement.

Being able to understand that the universe is vibrational in nature helps us comprehend how profound these subtler frequencies are and what a gift we have in recognizing them. We are here for a reason. Learning about our superpowers helps us begin to see how we can assist our family, friends, or organizations by providing profound insight. You are incredibly valuable. Your vision can create change. You are a force just by understanding your role at this time.

As we have learned about our own special abilities, we have started to deepen our understanding of consciousness. There is a bigger, subtler world and you have access to it. You are starting to understand the universe on a much deeper level and realize that your psychic spiritual self means that, because of your special modalities, you can experience that layer. You are not a freak, you just have the ability to see, hear, or touch the more subtle energies around you. This consciousness or awareness brings you closer to understanding and connecting with Source Energy. Source Energy is another way of saying "God." Religion sometimes gets in the way of understanding Source Energy, but it can also be comforting knowing that we are not really exploring beyond things that we have grown up to believe. Source energy is the vibration that goes beyond all that we can see. When we connect that energy with our inner being, there is nothing more satisfying. That is when we have clarity and can go forward with more confidence. We are acting in alignment and everything is possible.

The Law of Attraction is something that we think is imagined, but actually it is as real as gravity. Having that higher perspective allows the opportunity to see it. What we see and feel attracts like kinds of experiences. We are no longer victims when we are able to look more deeply at our own connection to what is happening. It gives us the chance to recognize our patterns and how we perpetuate them in reality. The Law of Attraction is at the heart of everything and we have more access to understanding because of our special "sight."

We also have learned how easy it is to pick up energies from others. That often, what we are experiencing is actually not even connected to us but rather stuff we've picked up along the way. Thought forms are real and we can hear them and also be susceptible to absorbing them from others. Because of this, we need to learn what belongs to us and what belongs to others so that we can release things back into the atmosphere. When we carry around too much of other people's energies, we don't feel good. We can get bogged down and feel heavy and anxious. It can cloud our vision and make us feel depressed and overwhelmed.

It is important to feel grounded. When we get overwhelmed it is a signal that we are carrying too much and need to practice our grounding exercises. We need to make a conscious decision to release what is not ours. Carrying around others' stuff is not helping them. It is just a burden. When we experience our own divine self, it uplifts others. Carrying around their baggage doesn't.

Walking in nature and doing conscious grounding exercises is the beginning to releasing things that are not ours.

There are some great ways to protect our energy using shields, white and gold light, and mirrors. When we are in public areas or going into something that can be toxic for us, knowing how to create these ways of protection can help keep us from absorbing unwanted energies. It is important to remember to use these tools in advance so that we can move forward with clarity.

The practice of gratitude also keeps our energies aligned on a high level, which helps us be less likely to absorb things on a more negative vibration. Gratitude can help us pivot from a downward spiral of negativity to keeping us grounded in the light. It helps us begin to see things from a more positive perspective. The practice of gratitude also creates a more positive outcome. As we have learned with the Law of Attraction, what we focus on becomes even more so. And if we are tuning in to the positive aspects around us we continue to create more of what we desire.

Beginning to create a regular meditation practice also helps us stay aligned to a higher vibration. It also lets us access our psychic abilities from a more grounded stance. It roots us to our own inner being and from there we have greater clarity. During our meditation we also have a greater access to our guidance system. We are more likely to receive messages that can be answers to questions we might have about direction or circumstances. Having a regular meditation practice also gives an ability to detach from events in order to regain a clearer perspective. We are able to give pause to reaction and to see things from a more balanced point of view. Meditation also has other physical benefits such as lowering our blood pressure and reducing stress. This is extremely helpful when we are feeling anxiety and absorbing too much energy from others. This is an opportunity each day to feel that connection so that we can release what isn't ours.

Because of our increased sensitivities to the energies around us, there are so many wonderful tools to help us on our journey. These tools are here to help us transform energies and keep us aligned in higher frequencies. Many of the tools are things we can carry unobtrusively so that we have magic in our pockets without drawing attention from others. We can pull them out whenever we need a boost. The more that you use these tools; the more you can know how to benefit from their properties.

Our families and friends may not be that open to our new discoveries about ourselves. It may threaten them and they may be condescending. That's why it is helpful to work with a therapist or join a support group as you start to learn how to expand your awareness and develop your skills. There has been a quiet battle inside where we have been afraid or uncertain about our special skills. Beginning to explore this part of ourselves in a safe environment can help us feel more at peace with who we are. This secret has taken a toll. Being out in the open in a safe place helps us figure out how we can work with our own special abilities.

You are here for a reason. You have come here to utilize your gifts for the benefit of humankind. It feels so good having access to all of your skills and to know those qualities that are *exceptional*! This is also just the beginning. There are so many wonderful resources. As you start to explore, you will learn how to develop your skills and deepen them with practice. Your intuition will only become stronger as you listen and pay attention.

You are unique. Although you may find that others share similarities in their skills, you are the one that is here for your purpose alone. You are here to bring light but also to create change. Having access to all of your skills is just the beginning. The rest is up to you.

Acknowledgments

I could never have written this book without the incredible support of my family.

To Robert, for his incredible strength, support, and patience, thank you for always wanting me to actualize my dreams. To my son Luke, who has asked profound questions about the universe since the day he was born. You have always encouraged me to learn more about almost everything as well as to understand the life of an empath. And to my daughter, Liv, you have pushed me to go outside my comfort zone and make a difference as well as keeping me up to speed with all of the new technology and social media! This team is the definition of love.

I also want to thank Dr. Angela Lauria and her team at the Difference Press and the Author Incubator for everything that they have done to support this process of making my dream come true. They are rock stars!

And finally, I want to thank Esther, Jerry and Abraham Hicks for all of their incredible support along the way.

About the Author

DEBORAH SUDARSKY is a Master Intuitive Coach. She is an author, successful entrepreneur, and motivational speaker. She has counseled hundreds of people, both in individual and group settings. She specializes in helping people find their special psychic gifts and feel safe, especially when they come from very traditional backgrounds. Currently, she is creating a network of support groups for those who wish to find their psychic gifts and live life to their full potential.

Deborah was en route to getting her Ph.D. in psychology before she had her first psychic reading, which changed her life. At that time, she was told that she was part of the Zuni Indian Guides and that she was to channel their energy in order to help others on their paths. From that point forward, she did readings and trained with some of the top leaders in their fields, including Polarity Therapy with Pierre Panatier, Cranial Sacral Therapy and Tuning Fork alignment with John Beaulieu, Shiatsu and Massage Therapy at the Ohashiatsu Institute, crystal healing, and working with DoTerra essential oils. After working with private clients and teaching, she decided to get some "real life" experience by working in television commercial production for a top award-winning company, BFCS. She decided to go back to school and get her master's degree in counseling with the intention of teaching meditation while counseling individual and groups in New York City Public School and a private girl's school in Brooklyn.

Deborah currently resides in Brooklyn, NY and Santa Monica, CA with her husband and Jack Russell Terrier, Lola. She loves spending time with her two children, is an advanced Scuba diver, and always enjoys the beach.

About Difference Press

Difference Press is the exclusive publishing arm of The Author Incubator, an educational company for entrepreneurs – including life coaches, healers, consultants, and community leaders – looking for a comprehensive solution to get their books written, published, and promoted. Its founder, Dr. Angela Lauria, has been bringing to life the literary ventures of hundreds of authors-in-transformation since 1994.

A boutique-style self-publishing service for clients of The Author Incubator, Difference Press boasts a fair and easy-to-understand profit structure, low-priced author copies, and author-friendly contract terms. Most importantly, all of our #incubatedauthors maintain ownership of their copyright at all times.

LET'S START A MOVEMENT WITH YOUR MESSAGE

In a market where hundreds of thousands of books are published every year and are never heard from again, The Author Incubator is different. Not only do all Difference Press books reach Amazon bestseller status, but also all of our authors are actively changing lives and making a difference.

Since launching in 2013, we've served over 500 authors who came to us with an idea for a book and were able to write it and get it self-published in less than 6 months. In addition, more than 100 of those books were picked up by traditional publishers and are now available in bookstores. We do this by selecting the highest quality and highest potential applicants for our future programs.

Our program doesn't only teach you how to write a book – our team of coaches, developmental editors, copy editors, art directors, and marketing experts incubate you from having a book idea to being a published, bestselling author, ensuring that the book you create can actually make a difference in the world. Then we give you the training you need to use your book to make the difference in the world, or to create a business out of serving your readers.

ARE YOU READY TO MAKE A DIFFERENCE?

You've seen other people make a difference with a book. Now it's your turn. If you are ready to stop watching and start taking massive action, go to http://theauthorincubator.com/apply/

"Yes, I'm ready!"

Thank You

I am so appreciative of your decision to explore your psychic gifts and learn more about who you are and why you are here. The fact that you have gotten this far lets me know that you are excited about your journey and I am thrilled for you! It also means that you are ready to begin to practice some of the tools in the book and explore areas that may resonate with you.

After you start to incorporate a meditation practice and a journal of gratitude, you will begin to feel a total increase in joy. Keep at it! Meditating takes some experimenting until you find the way that works best for you. Start slowly and increase the amount of time, as you feel comfortable. The benefits are enormous. The decision to find aspects of appreciation in your gratitude journal has immediate benefits. It really does shift the energy when you are feeling down or afraid. I can't recommend it enough.

To support you on your path of embracing your psychic gifts, I have created an EXCEPTIONAL ASSESSMENT just for you. It's a simple diagnostic assessment to help you figure out next steps for your journey. You can find it at: **EmbraceYourPsychicGifts.com.**

I would love to hear your stories and anything that you have discovered by reading the book and for more information email me at **DeborahSudarsky@gmail.com.**